PIANO • VOCAL • GUITAR

UPDATED EDITION

The Illustrated Treasury of

SONGS

HYPERION

NEW YORK

HAL•LEONARD®
CORPORATION

7777 W. BLUEMOUND RD. P.O. BOX 13819 MILWAUKEE, WI 53213

The following songs are the property of:

BOURNE CO.
New York
Music Publishers
5 West 37th Street
New York, NY 10018

Baby Mine
Give A Little Whistle
Heigh-Ho
Hi-Diddle-Dee-Dee (An Actor's Life For Me)
I'm Wishing
I've Got No Strings
Some Day My Prince Will Come
When I See An Elephant Fly
When You Wish Upon A Star
Whistle While You Work
Who's Afraid Of The Big Bad Wolf?

Copyright © 1998, Disney Enterprises, Inc.

Copublished in 1998 by Hal Leonard Corporation,
Milwaukee, Wisconsin and Hyperion, New York, New York

ISBN 0-7868-6456-7

FIRST EDITION
10 9 8 7 6 5 4 3 2 1

Printed in Hong Kong

CONTENTS

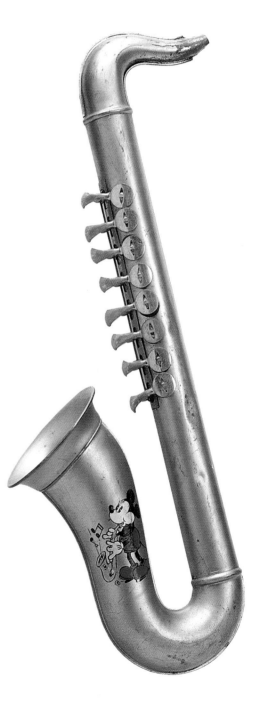

INTRODUCTION

Walt Disney didn't read or write music. In fact, he never even played an instrument, unless you count an unsuccessful stab at the violin during grade school in Kansas City.

And yet his influence upon music was, and continues to be, so profound that the great American composer Jerome Kern was moved to say, "Disney has made use of music as language. In the synchronization of humorous episodes with humorous music, he has unquestionably given us the outstanding contribution of our time."

That's lofty praise, especially coming as it did from a musical legend like Kern. But what makes his words all the more amazing is the fact that he said them in 1936, *before* the release of *Snow White and the Seven Dwarfs*, arguably one of Walt Disney's greatest moments not only in animation, but music as well.

Still, the question remains: if Walt didn't write any songs or compose any scores, how could he have had such a deep and lasting impact on music?

The answer, simply enough, is the same way in which he had such a profound effect upon animation without so much as drawing even one mouse or dwarf.

Walt was the mover and shaker, the man of vision who gathered around him some of the most talented writers, artists, composers and musicians, who bought into his dreams and schemes and made them happen, all under his watchful eye.

"There's a terrific power to music. You can run any of these pictures and they'd be dragging and boring, but the minute you put music behind them, they have life and vitality they don't get any other way."

–Walt Disney

Walt and Roy Disney with the special "Oscar" awarded to Walt in 1932 for the creation of Mickey Mouse.

Disney's imprimatur is stamped onto every song . . .

He once described his role this way:

> My role? Well, you know I was stumped one day when a little boy asked, "Do you draw Mickey Mouse?" I had to admit I do not draw anymore. "Then you think up the jokes and ideas?" "No," I said, "I don't do that." Finally, he looked at me and said, "Mr. Disney, just what do you do?" "Well," I said, "sometimes I think of myself as a little bee. I go from one area of the Studio to another and gather pollen and sort of stimulate everybody. I guess that's the job I do."

Of course, that doesn't explain Walt Disney's uncanny feel for what worked and what didn't, be it in music, films or theme parks. Perhaps Eric Sevareid summed it up best in his tribute to Walt on the *CBS Evening News* the day Disney died: "He was an original; not just an American original, but an original, period. He was a happy accident; one of the happiest this century has experienced . . . . People are saying we'll never see his like again."

Maybe it was his Midwestern upbringing and mid-American, mainstream appreciation for music and movies, or maybe he *was* just "a happy accident," but Walt Disney aimed to create entertainment that he himself would enjoy. Could he help it if hundreds of millions of people around the world happened to agree with him?

So although he didn't write "When You Wish Upon a Star," "Zip-A-Dee-Doo-Dah" or any of the other hundreds of tunes that make up the Disney canon, his imprimatur is stamped onto every song and score. When you hear "Whistle While You Work," you may not know that the words were written by Larry Morey and the music by Frank Churchill, but you certainly know it's a Disney song.

It didn't matter what a composer's background was, whether he was a honky-tonk pianist from Los Angeles, a jingle writer from New York's Tin Pan Alley or a pop star from England, when he wrote for Walt Disney he wrote in a style that was, consciously or not, immediately recognizable not as his own, but as Walt Disney's.

"No matter what I or anyone else in the music department wrote, people always recognized it as being the 'Disney sound,'" says Buddy Baker, a longtime Disney staff composer. "But if I was asked to define the Disney sound or how we got it, I would have to answer that I didn't know. It's not something I thought about while I was writing the music.

"I think a clue to the Disney sound, though, comes from the man himself," he adds. "Walt Disney had a wonderful concept of what the music should be, which is a great clue for the composer. For instance, if he wanted a big, symphonic score, he'd tell you that and he'd even tell you what he'd want it to sound like."

Disney songs represent a style and sprightliness that make them eminently hummable and totally unforgettable. They were very much a reflection of their patron, who concentrated on melody and didn't like anything that was too loud or high-pitched.

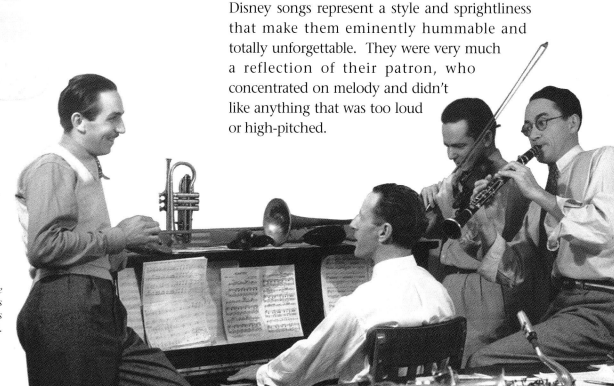

Music lightens a story session in the mid-1930s as Walt Disney visits (from left) Webb Smith, Ted Sears and Pinto Colvig.

Even the "Disney" songs and scores being written today, a whole quarter of a century after Walt Disney's death, reflect the spirit and influence of this man who had a special ability to recognize what kind of music best fit a scene or situation and, more importantly (and more to the point), what was good.

It was Walt's direction and influence that led his composers and musicians to pioneer musical concepts and technologies that influenced both the film and music industries for decades – and continue to do so to this day.

But the music didn't start out as Disney's own. In the first several Mickey Mouse cartoons, produced in 1928 and 1929, the music was either borrowed or adapted. An example was Mickey's very first cartoon, *Steamboat Willie*, released in November, 1928, and featuring the songs "Steamboat Bill" and "Turkey in the Straw."

(Top) Walt Disney's classic portrait with Mickey Mouse, taken at the Disney Studios on Hyperion Avenue in the 1930's. (Right) In 1938, Disney purchased undeveloped property in Burbank, which soon became the permanent home to the new Walt Disney Studios.

Walt created entertainment that he himself would enjoy

Still, even if the music wasn't written by members of Walt's staff, it was arranged in such a way that it sounded as if it just might have been. For instance, "Steamboat Bill," written in 1910, was whistled by the mouse himself during the opening moments of the cartoon.

THE EARLY YEARS

The sound that played the key role in Disney cartoons was music.

"Turkey in the Straw," which dates as far back as 1834 and is arguably a sing-song classic in the tradition of "Camptown Races" and "My Darling Clementine," was not arranged for normal instruments, such as guitars, flutes or pianos, but was instead configured to accommodate the variety of "instruments" Mickey plays during the cartoon, including a washboard, pots and pans, a cat, a duck, several suckling pigs and a cow's teeth. ("Turkey in the Straw," by the way, was selected for *Steamboat Willie* because it was one of the only tunes a young assistant animator named Wilfred Jackson, the sole musician at the small Disney Studios, could play on the harmonica.)

It could be said that the Disney musical legacy actually did begin with Walt himself. In 1929, he teamed with his then-musical director Carl Stalling to write a song that would become an anthem of sorts for his already famous star, Mickey Mouse.

That song, "Minnie's Yoo Hoo," was first heard in the 1929 short "Mickey's Follies." It is the only song for which Walt Disney ever took a writing credit.

Mickey Mouse and the musical improvisation that made him famous in his debut film, Steamboat Willie.

But that doesn't mean Walt didn't play an active role in the creation of the music heard in all succeeding Disney Studio cartoon shorts and animated features. He simply entrusted it to more accomplished composers and arrangers, the first of which was Stalling, an old friend from Kansas City.

Mickey Mouse shorts. Walt wanted Stalling to fit the music to the action, while Stalling felt the action should fit the music.

The Silly Symphonies were a compromise. In the Mickey cartoons, the music would continue to play second fiddle to the characters and the action, but in the Silly Symphonies the music would rule.

Stalling stayed with the Studio less than two years, jumping from Silly Symphonies at Disney to Looney Tunes and Merrie Melodies at Warner Brothers, where he created his own musical legacy composing scores for the likes of Bugs Bunny, Daffy Duck and Porky Pig.

Despite Stalling's departure, the Silly Symphonies continued. In fact, they became so popular that Walt Disney began beefing up his music staff in the early '30s to handle the increased need for music for them.

In "Silly Symphonies" the music would rule

It was Stalling who persuaded Walt to begin the Silly Symphony cartoon series, which grew out of disagreements the two had over the use of music in the

The surprise hit song from Three Little Pigs *spawned a range of merchandise, including (left to right) sheet music, a board game, and records. These rare 1933 items are treasured by collectors today.*

One of the composers he hired was Frank Churchill, a young musician who had studied at UCLA and gained experience playing honky-tonk piano in Mexico and peforming on a Los Angeles radio station (as well as serving as a session player in recording sessions for Disney cartoons). This heretofore unsung musician would play an important role in Disney music over the next decade. And he started off with a bang, writing Disney's first big hit, a song that came out of the most famous of the Silly Symphonies, *Three Little Pigs*.

Released in 1933 during the depths of the Depression, *Three Little Pigs* and its famous song, "Who's Afraid of the Big Bad Wolf?," provided hope and humor to a country that was badly in need of both.

As with many Disney films, *Three Little Pigs* comes from a children's story. But to Churchill, it also represented real life. While growing up on his family's ranch in San Luis Obispo, California, he was given three piglets to raise by his mother. All went well until a real "Big Bad Wolf" killed one of them.

As legend has it, when Churchill was asked to write a song for the cartoon, he recalled his horrifying childhood experience and penned "Who's Afraid of the Big Bad Wolf?" in about five minutes, patterning the song loosely on "Happy Birthday." When it was released as a single and in sheet music, it featured additional lyrics by Ann Ronell.

"Who's Afraid of the Big Bad Wolf?" provided hope and humor to a country that was badly in need of both.

With "Who's Afraid of the Big Bad Wolf?" Walt Disney and his staff had created their first sing-a-long classic. It certainly wasn't going to be their last.

In 1929, the Disney Studio's creative team included (standing from left) Johnny Cannon, Walt Disney, Bert Gillett, Ub Iwerks, Wilfred Jackson, Les Clark; (seated from left) Carl Stalling, Jack King and Ben Sharpsteen.

A COMING OF AGE

The next step for Walt and his staff was the creation of the first full-length animated feature. But Walt wasn't content to "just" create and produce a feature-length cartoon. He envisioned something more.

From its beginnings, *Snow White and the Seven Dwarfs* was planned around music. However, early attempts at songs did not satisfy Walt. He complained that they were too much in the vein of so many Hollywood musicals that introduced songs without regard to the story. "We should set a new pattern, a new way to use music," he told his staff. "Weave it into the story so somebody doesn't just burst into song."

That last line, as simply stated as it is, has been the guiding principle in Disney animated features from *Snow White* and *Pinocchio* all the way through the more recent efforts, including *Beauty and the Beast, Aladdin* and *The Lion King*.

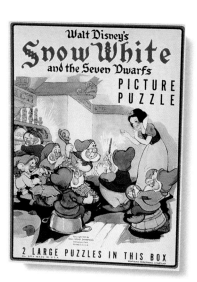

What Walt wanted with *Snow White and the Seven Dwarfs* was something closer to Broadway musical than Hollywood motion picture.

Frank Churchill and Larry Morey were assigned the task of writing the songs for *Snow White*. By the time all was said and sung, the pair had written 25 songs, only eight of which ended up in the film. But what an eight they were, each one a classic in its own right.

The first original motion picture soundtrack record album was Snow White and the Seven Dwarfs, *released by Victor Records in 1937.*

"We should set a new pattern, a new way to use music"

Walt Disney didn't write any songs for *Snow White*, but he played an active role in defining the content of each song and how it would fit into the film, as these notes from a story conference on "Whistle While You Work" demonstrate:

> Change words of song so they fit in more with Snow White's handing the animals brushes, etc. Snow White: "If you just hum a merry tune"…and they start humming. Then Snow White would start to tell them to "whistle while you work." She would start giving the animals things to do. By that time, she has sung, of course… Birds would come marching in. Try to arrange to stay with the birds for a section of whistling. Orchestra would play with a whistling effect…get it in the woodwinds…like playing something instrumentally to sound like whistling…

> Get a way to finish the song that isn't just an end. Work in a shot trucking [moving] out of the house. Truck back and show animals shaking rugs out of the windows…little characters outside beating things out in the yard…

> Truck out and the melody of "Whistle While You Work" gets quieter and quieter. Leave them all working. The last thing you see as you truck away is little birds hanging out clothes. Fade out on that and music would fade out. At the end, all you would hear is the flute — before fading into the "Dig Dig" song [which precedes the song "Heigh-Ho"] and the hammering rhythm.

Snow White and the Seven Dwarfs ushered in not only the Golden Age of Disney Animation in the late 1930s and early 1940s, but the Golden Age of Disney Music as well. While Disney's animators were creating some of the most beautiful screen images ever seen, the studio's composers were producing some of the most memorable songs ever heard, including "When You Wish Upon a Star" from *Pinocchio* (1940), "Baby Mine" from *Dumbo* (1941) and "Little April Shower" from *Bambi* (1942).

World War II brought an abrupt end to the Golden Age. At the Disney Studios, the emphasis changed from creating animated features to producing cartoon shorts and instructional films to aid the war effort. Even after the war was over, Walt Disney didn't immediately return to animated features. Instead, he concentrated on "package" pictures (movies that featured a series of animated shorts rolled into one motion picture) and films featuring both live action and animation.

But Disney's staff of composers continued to play a significant role in these efforts, writing such memorable tunes as the Latin-influenced "Saludos Amigos" and "You Belong to My Heart" from the two South American travelog-style films *Saludos Amigos* (1943) and *The Three Caballeros* (1945), "The Lord Is Good to Me" from *Melody Time* (1948) and one of the most popular Disney songs ever written, "Zip-A-Dee-Doo-Dah," the irresistibly upbeat tune from *Song of the South* (1946).

Composer Frank Churchill (left) and sequence director/lyricist Larry Morey in the mid-1930s creating songs for Snow White and the Seven Dwarfs.

SONGS FROM TIN PAN ALLEY

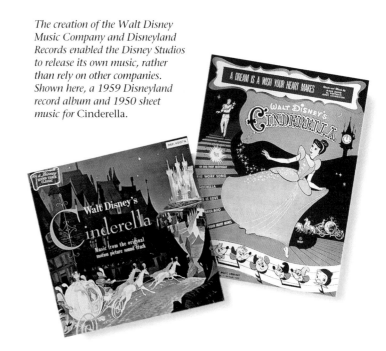

The creation of the Walt Disney Music Company and Disneyland Records enabled the Disney Studios to release its own music, rather than rely on other companies. Shown here, a 1959 Disneyland record album and 1950 sheet music for Cinderella.

In 1950, Walt Disney returned to animated features with the release of *Cinderella*, but instead of relying on his music staff for the film's song score, he turned to writers from New York's Tin Pan Alley, something he would continue to do for his animated features throughout the 1950s.

Originally 28th Street in Manhattan, Tin Pan Alley was home to many of the largest song publishers in the United States. Each publisher employed an army of songwriters, who worked out of small offices furnished with nothing more than pianos and music stands. During the summer, the writers would open their windows in a futile effort to get some relief from the stifling New York heat (the buildings weren't air conditioned). The noise of the pianos echoing through the street gave one the impression of people banging on tin pans, hence the name "Tin Pan Alley."

Walt didn't consciously set out to use Tin Pan Alley writers for *Cinderella*. While in New York on business prior to the start of production, he kept hearing on the radio a catchy novelty song, "Chi-Baba Chi-Baba," written by the team of Mack David, Jerry Livingston and Al Hoffman. He was so taken with the song that he ended up hiring the trio to write the songs for *Cinderella*. Perhaps it's no surprise, then, that one of the songs, "Bibbidi Bobbidi Boo," is in the same vein as "Chi-Baba."

Walt again turned to Tin Pan Alley for *Alice in Wonderland* (1951), primarily because he felt the film would need an abundance of novelty songs, something the Tin Pan Alley gang was quite adept at producing. In all, 14 songs were written for *Alice*, including "I'm Late," one of nine tunes written for the film by Bob Hilliard and Sammy Fain, and "The Unbirthday Song" contributed by the *Cinderella* trio of David, Hoffman and Livingston.

The renaissance in Disney animation continued through the 1950s and early 1960s with the release of such animated features as *Peter Pan* (1953), *Lady and the Tramp* (1955), *Sleeping Beauty* (1959) and *101 Dalmatians* (1961). The bulk of the songs continued to be written by Tin Pan Alley tunesmiths, such as Sammy Cahn, Sammy Fain and Jack Lawrence. The notable exception was *Lady and the Tramp*, which featured songs by Peggy Lee and Sonny Burke.

The increasing reliance on outside writers for songs for the animated features presented no danger to the jobs of Disney's crack staff of composers and arrangers. At least they didn't seem worried by it, perhaps because they were so busy.

[The 1950s were] a hectic time at the Studio," recalls Buddy Baker, who joined the Disney music staff following a career in big bands and radio, "We had the weekly series [*Disneyland*, which later became *The Wonderful World of Disney*, among other titles] to write music for, plus the daily show [*The Mickey Mouse Club*]. This was in addition to the feature films the Studio was producing. And Walt demanded quality, whether it was music for a multi-million dollar animated feature or a television show."

Walt's staff of composers was so busy writing the music they often turned to anyone who was ready, willing and able to write the lyrics, be they animators, scriptwriters, story editors or, in the case of "Old Yeller," Studio nurses (the lyrics for that song are credited to Gil George, who was in fact Disney Studio nurse Hazel George).

Disney staffers at the time included music director Oliver Wallace ("Old Yeller," and "Pretty Irish Girl"), Jimmie Dodd ("The Mickey Mouse March") and George Bruns ("Zorro" and "The Ballad of Davy Crockett").

Bruns' experience writing "The Ballad of Davy Crockett" for the *Davy Crockett* series of TV shows was typical of the way songs were written for Walt Disney in the harried '50s, though the results were far from typical.

"Walt needed what I call a little 'throwaway' tune that would bridge the time gaps in the story of Davy Crockett," recalled Bruns. "He needed a song that would carry the story from one sequence to another. I threw together the melody line and chorus, 'Davy, Davy Crockett, King of the Wild Frontier,' in about 30 minutes."

Tom Blackburn, the scriptwriter for the *Davy Crockett* series, had never before written a song, but that didn't stop him from adding the lyrics, 120 lines of them (the completed version has 20 stanzas of six lines each).

Composer George Bruns created a diverse range of music for Disney, from the award-winning score for Sleeping Beauty *to the hit song "The Ballad of Davy Crockett."*

Even before the television series went on the air, "The Ballad of Davy Crockett" took the country by storm. Bruns and Blackburn's little "throwaway" tune became a national sensation, much as coonskin caps would when the show premiered.

"It certainly took everybody at the Studio by surprise," said Bruns. "The irony of it was that most people thought it was an authentic folk song that we had uncovered and updated. Usually when you have a hit song, there are always lawsuits claiming prior authorship. In the case of 'Davy Crockett,' not a single suit was filed."

"The Ballad of Davy Crockett" became the fastest-selling record of 1955.

THE SHERMANS MARCH THROUGH DISNEY

Perhaps the greatest achievement of the Sherman Brothers' Disney career came in 1964 with the release of *Mary Poppins*, for which they wrote 14 songs and earned two Academy Awards, one for Best Song ("Chim-Chim-Cheree") and the other for Best Song Score.

"Writing songs for *Mary Poppins* was a songwriter's dream. Each song we did had a purpose, a reason for being," says Robert Sherman, echoing the long-held philosophy of Walt Disney about music in motion pictures.

Typical of their experiences composing tunes for *Mary Poppins* was the inspiration behind one of the most popular and memorable tunes in the film, "Supercalifragilisticexpialidocious."

I**f the 1950s were characterized by Walt Disney's reliance on Tin Pan Alley songwriters, the trend in the 1960s could be summed up in two words: Sherman Brothers.

Hired by Walt Disney in 1961 as staff songwriters, Richard M. and Robert B. Sherman proved versatile and prolific during their almost decade-long association with Disney, writing more than 200 songs, many of which have become timeless classics.

"When we were little boys in summer camp in the Catskill Mountains in the mid-1930s," explains Richard Sherman, "we heard this word. Not the exact word, but a word very similar to 'supercal.' It was a word that was longer than 'antidisestablishmentarianism,' and it gave us kids a word that no adult had. It was our own

"Supercalifragilisticexpialidocious"

The pair penned songs for animated features (*The Sword in the Stone* [1963], *The Jungle Book* [1967], *The Aristocats* [1970]) and featurettes (*Winnie the Pooh and the Honey Tree* [1966]), live-action musicals (*Summer Magic* [1963], *The Happiest Millionaire* [1967]), live-action non-musicals (*The Parent Trap* [1961], *In Search of the Castaways* [1962], *The Monkey's Uncle* [1965], *That Darn Cat* [1965]), musicals combining live-action and animation (*Bedknobs and Broomsticks* [1971]), theme parks (*The Enchanted Tiki Room* [1963]), and even the New York World's Fair (*Carousel of Progress*, *It's a Small World* [1964]).

special word, and we wanted the Banks children to have that same feeling."

Songwriters Richard Sherman (left) and Robert Sherman (right) review the music for Mary Poppins *with the film's co-producer and writer, Bill Walsh (center).*

*Dick Van Dyke,
Karen Dotrice,
Matthew Garber
and Julie Andrews
in Mary Poppins.*

Mary Poppins also proved to be the crowning achievement of Walt Disney's long and storied career. Combining live-action, animation and the Sherman Brothers song score, it was the culmination of everything he'd been working toward in his more than 40 years in the film business.

When Walt Disney passed away on December 15, 1966, there was concern that his studio would not be able to survive without him. But Walt had confidence it would. "I think by this time my staff...[is] convinced that Walt is right, that quality will out," he once said. "And so I think they're going to stay with that policy because it's proved that

it's a good business policy... I think they're convinced and I think they'll hang on, as you say, after Disney."

Throughout the 1970s and 1980s the Disney Studios continued producing animated and live-action features, but all of them, with the exceptions of *Robin Hood* (1973) and *Pete's Dragon* (1977), were non-musicals. That didn't mean there weren't *any* songs in Disney movies. Such animated features as *The Rescuers* (1977) and *The Fox and the Hound* (1981) did feature songs, but these songs were usually performed during the opening or closing credits and were not essential to the story.

A MUSICAL RENAISSANCE

"Animation is the last great place to do Broadway musicals," said Ashman, explaining the inspiration for *The Little Mermaid* (1989), *Beauty and the Beast* (1991) and *Aladdin* (1992). "It's a place you can use a whole other set of skills and a way of working which is more the way plays and musicals are made. With most films, the story seems to come first and the songs are an afterthought.

"Coming from a musical theater background," he continued, "Alan and I are used to writing songs for characters in situations. For *The Little Mermaid* we wanted songs that would really move the story forward and keep things driving ahead."

The seven songs Ashman and Menken wrote for the film did that and more. The result was the beginning of a New Golden Age of Animation that continues to this day.

Ashman and Menken followed the success of *The Little Mermaid* (for which they won an Academy Award for "Under the Sea") with *Beauty and the Beast*.

A review of the film in *Newsweek* magazine says it all: "The most delicious musical score of 1991 is Alan Menken and Howard Ashman's *Beauty and the Beast*. If the growing armada of

All that changed in 1988 with the release of *Oliver & Company*, Disney's first full-scale animated musical in more than a decade.

The film featured five tunes written by a Who's Who of pop songwriters, including Barry Manilow, Dan Hartman and Dean Pitchford. But the key was that all of the songs adhered to an old Disney maxim: music should play an integral and prominent part in the story without overshadowing or disrupting it.

"Music should come out of the dialogue," said the film's director, George Scribner, reemphasizing a point Walt Disney had made many times many years before. "The best

"Animation is the last great place to do Broadway musicals."

music advances the story or defines a character. The challenge was to figure out areas in our film where music could better express a concept or idea."

Perhaps no one knew this better than a New York-based lyricist named Howard Ashman, who co-wrote "Once Upon a Time in New York City" for *Oliver & Company*.

With his longtime writing partner Alan Menken, Ashman redefined and revitalized the animated musical, bringing to it a style, wit and sophistication that hadn't been seen or heard since the early 1940s.

titanically troubled Broadway musicals had half its charm and affectionate cleverness, the ships wouldn't be foundering."

The duo wrote six songs for the film, including an unprecedented three songs that were nominated for Academy Awards, "Be Our Guest" "Belle" and the eventual Oscar-winner "Beauty and the Beast."

Ariel and friends in The Little Mermaid.

Before his death in March of 1991, Ashman had written lyrics for three songs in the next big Disney animated feature, *Aladdin*, including "Friend Like Me." Once again, the composer was Alan Menken. For the rest of the score Menken collaborated with lyricist Tim Rice, a theater veteran who, earlier in his career, wrote *Evita* and *Jesus Christ Superstar* with Andrew Lloyd Webber. Menken, Rice, and the film were honored with an Academy Award for Best Song for "A Whole New World."

The songwriting team of Howard Ashman (left) and Alan Menken received Academy Awards for their work on The Little Mermaid *and* Beauty and the Beast.

Disney's live-action musical tradition continued with the 1992 release of *Newsies*, a full-scale production about the organization of newsboys in New York early in the 20th century. The score, by Alan Menken and Jack Feldman, includes the boys' inspirational anthem, "Seize the Day."

As the 1990s continued, Disney definitely reaffirmed its place as the world's best producer of beautiful and successful animated films. The next animated musical, released in 1994, was the universally beloved *The Lion King*, the allegorical story of the love between a lion cub and his father. Tim Rice was signed first to write the lyrics. "The studio asked me if I had any suggestions as to who could write the music. They said, 'Choose anybody in the world and choose the best.' I said, 'Well, Elton John would be fantastic.'" The producers were at first hesitant to approach the legendary rock star, but as it turned out, he was anxious to come on board. "I actually jumped at the chance," John confessed, "because I knew that Disney was a class act and I liked the story line and the people immediately."

Has there ever been a musical number on film, live or animated, that surpasses the emotional beauty of the the opening number, "Circle of Life"? Rice, who first wrote the words for the song, was amazed at the speed with which Elton John composed. "I gave him the lyrics at the beginning of the session at about two in the afternoon. By half past three, he'd finished writing and recording a stunning demo." Disney added another Academy Award to its collection when "Can You Feel the Love Tonight?" was cited as Best Song.

Pocahontas was the first Disney animated feature inspired by factual history. It brought another major theater talent into the Disney studios in Stephen Schwartz, who wrote the lyrics for the score, with music once again by Alan Menken. Schwartz knew success at a young age on Broadway as the composer and lyricist of *Godspell* and *Pippin*. The combined talents of Menken and Schwartz produced yet another Academy Award for Best Song for "Colors of the Wind," a chart-topping hit for singer Vanessa Williams.

Toy Story, the first full-length feature film animated entirely on computers, takes place among the magical lives of a six-year-old's collection of toys. A special film like this needed a unique kind of song, and Disney found that in singer-songwriter Randy Newman. "You've Got a Friend in Me" is the chummy song that expresses the easy goodwill of the enchanting story of Woody, Buzz and Andy.

Alan Menken's sixth score for Disney was another collaboration with Stephen Schwartz — the adaptation of the classic 19th century Victor Hugo novel *The Hunchback of Notre Dame*. This was an incredibly ambitious undertaking in every regard. Just the task of adapting a screenplay from the sprawling novel is difficult enough, but creating a satisfying animated musical from this complicated story was a monumental task. The resulting critically acclaimed film is evidence of just how splendidly all those involved succeeded. The score contains an extensive, expressive collection of songs borrowing influences from gypsy music, French music, and traditional liturgical music. The richly emotional songs include "God Help the Outcasts," which, beyond the film score was recorded by Bette Midler, and "Someday," which became a hit for the vocal group All-4-One.

For *Hercules* Disney turned to a new source for a story: ancient Greek mythology. But this was no dull classroom textbook topic as realized by Disney studios. The film is a marvelously entertaining tale of the triumph of a true hero, enlivened by new songs, once again by Alan Menken, with lyrics by David Zippel, a Tony Award–winner for his work on the Broadway musical *City of Angels*. Rock singer Michael Bolton had a hit single with the expansive, soaring "Go the Distance," certainly an anthem befitting the mighty son of Zeus.

Nearly ten years ago Disney created an animation studio in Orlando, Walt Disney Feature Animation Florida. *Mulan* is the first feature film largely created there using amazing state-of-the-art computer-assisted animation. This 2,000-year-old tale is of a courageous young Chinese woman who enters the army disguised as a man so that her ailing father can be spared military service. Technology allowed panoramic camera effects never before possible in animation, especially amazing crowd scenes, and the attack of the Huns. The songs, by Matthew Wilder and David Zippel, include "Reflection," and "Honor to Us All."

One of the most exciting developments at Disney has been the expansion of the company's empire to include Broadway musicals. *Beauty and the Beast* was adapted for the stage in vivid fashion, with additional music and lyrics by Alan Menken and Tim Rice. The show opened on Broadway on April 18, 1994, and at this writing is still a hot ticket. A touring company of the musical has been a smash success on the road.

Disney's claim to a piece of Broadway became even more tangible with the acquisition and renovation of the New Amsterdam Theatre, built in 1903, restored to its original splendor, now a cornerstone in the major redevelopment of 42nd Street in New York. The New Amsterdam is home to *The Lion King: The Broadway Musical*, one of the most innovative musicals ever to open on the great white way. The stage adaptation from the animated film opened on Broadway on November 13, 1997, and contains additional songs by Elton John and Tim Rice, as well as music by Hanz Zimmer, Lebo M, Marck Mancina, and Jay Rifkin. The stunning production was directed by cutting-edge talent Julie Taymor. The musical won the 1998 Tony Award for Best Musical, and is the biggest hit New York has seen in many years, with sold-out houses booked many months in advance.

Members of the "Mickey Mouse Club" in a group shot with Walt Disney.

Perhaps it was Walt Disney himself who summed up best the reasons for the important role and the incredible success music has enjoyed in Disney animated features, live-action motion pictures and theme parks:

"Music has always had a prominent part in all our products from the early cartoon days. So much so, in fact, that I cannot think of the pictorial story without thinking about the complementary music that will fulfill it ... I have had no formal musical training. But by long experience and by strong personal leaning, I've selected musical themes, original or adapted, that were guided to wide audience acceptance.

But credit for the memorable songs and scores must, of course, go to the brilliant composers and musicians who have been associated with me through the years."

Minnie's Yoo Hoo

From Walt Disney's *Mickey's Follies*

Words by WALT DISNEY and CARL STALLING
Music by CARL STALLING

Who's Afraid Of The Big Bad Wolf?

From Walt Disney's *Three Little Pigs*

Words and Music by FRANK CHURCHILL
Additional Lyric by ANN RONELL

Slowly

Who's a-fraid of the big bad wolf, big bad wolf, big bad wolf? Who's a-fraid of the

big bad wolf? Tra la la la la. Who's a-fraid of the big bad wolf,

big bad wolf, big bad wolf? Who's a-fraid of the big bad wolf? Tra la la la

Heigh-Ho

The Dwarfs' Marching Song
From Walt Disney's
Snow White And The Seven Dwarfs

Words by LARRY MOREY
Music by FRANK CHURCHILL

March tempo

We dig dig dig dig dig dig dig in our mine the whole day thru.
dig dig dig dig dig dig dig and we try to do our bit.

To dig dig dig dig dig dig dig is what we like to do.
We dig dig dig dig dig dig dig un - til it's time to quit.

And while we dig we
And then we war - ble

32

34

I'm Wishing

From Walt Disney's *Snow White And The Seven Dwarfs*

Words by LARRY MOREY
Music by FRANK CHURCHILL

It's so sad and lone - ly, wish - ing well, _____

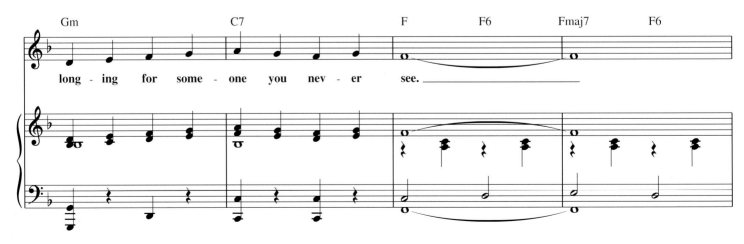

long - ing for some - one you nev - er see. _____

Some Day My Prince Will Come

From Walt Disney's
Snow White And The Seven Dwarfs

Words by LARRY MOREY
Music by FRANK CHURCHILL

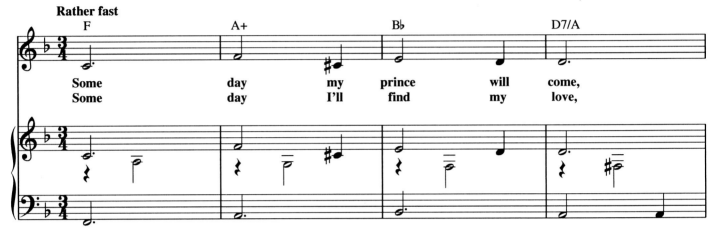

Some day my prince will come,
Some day I'll find my love,

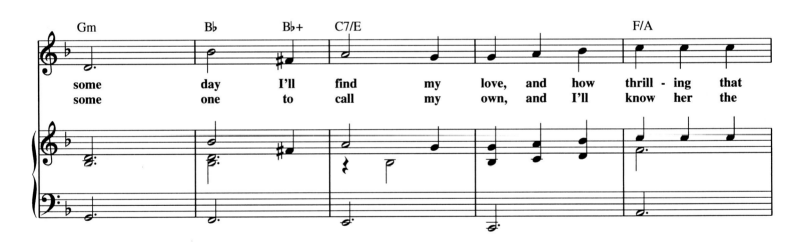

some day I'll find my love, and how thrill-ing that
some one to call my own, and I'll know her that the

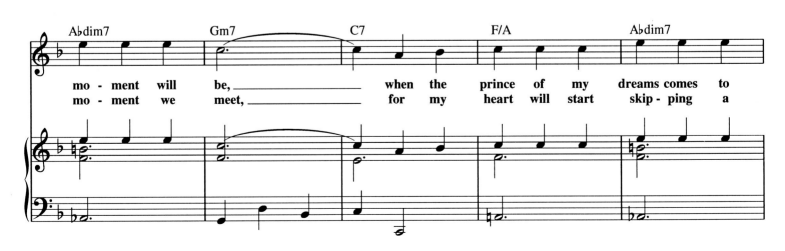

mo-ment will be,_____ when the prince of my dreams comes to
mo-ment we meet,_____ for my heart will start skip-ping a

Whistle While You Work

From Walt Disney's
Snow White And The Seven Dwarfs

Words by LARRY MOREY
Music by FRANK CHURCHILL

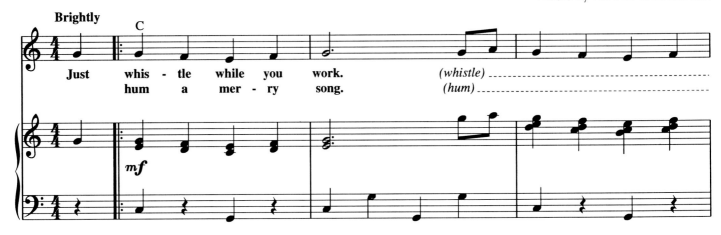

Just whis - tle while you work. *(whistle)* _____
hum a mer - ry song. *(hum)* _____

Put on that grin and start right in to
Just do your best and then take a rest and

whis - tle loud and long. Just
sing your - self a

song. When there's too much to

Give A Little Whistle

From Walt Disney's *Pinocchio*

Words by NED WASHINGTON
Music by LEIGH HARLINE

Hi-Diddle-Dee-dee

(An Actor's Life For Me)
From Walt Disney's *Pinocchio*

Words by NED WASHINGTON
Music by LEIGH HARLINE

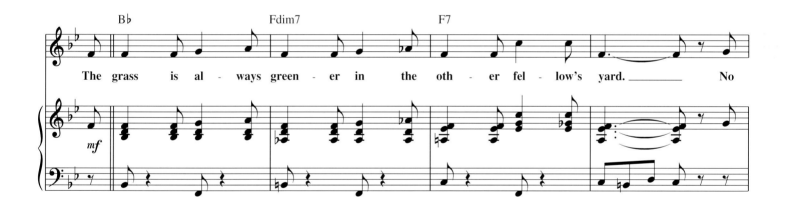

The grass is al - ways green - er in the oth - er fel - low's yard. _____ No

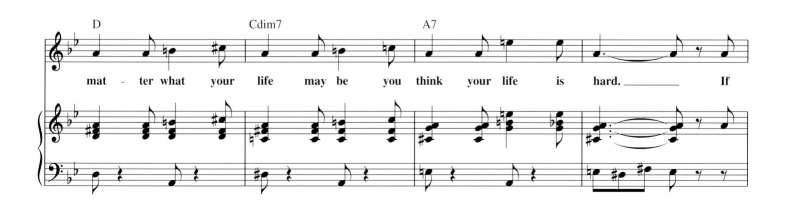

mat - ter what your life may be you think your life is hard. _____ If

46

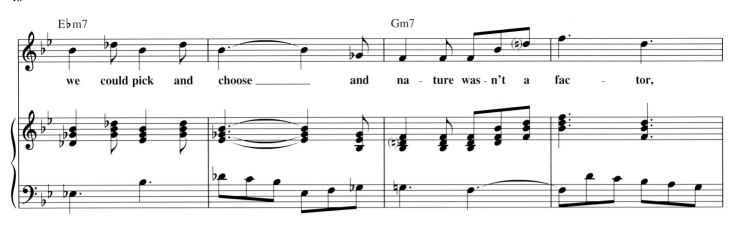

we could pick and choose _____ and na - ture was - n't a fac - tor,

here's a bit of news: _____ I'd pick the life of an act - or.

Hi - did - dle - dee - dee, _____ an act - or's life for me, _____ a

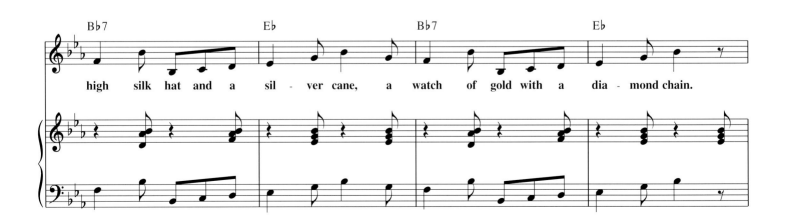

high silk hat and a sil - ver cane, a watch of gold with a dia - mond chain.

Hi - did - dle - dee - doo, _____ you sleep till af - ter

two. _____ You prom - e - nade with a big cig - ar, you

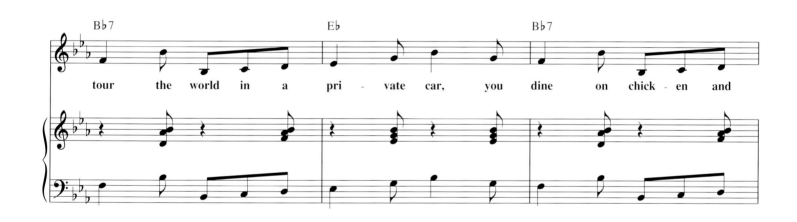

tour the world in a pri - vate car, you dine on chick - en and

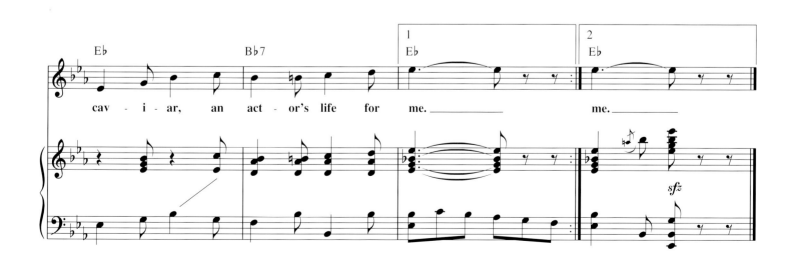

cav - i - ar, an act - or's life for me. _____ me. _____

I've Got No Strings

From Walt Disney's *Pinocchio*

Words by NED WASHINGTON
Music by LEIGH HARLINE

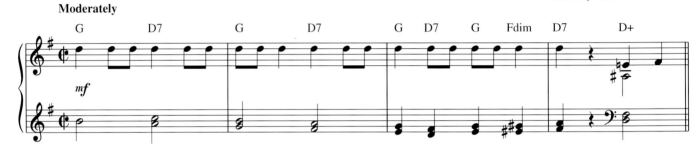

Why does the gay lit-tle dick-y bird sing? What put the "zing" in a

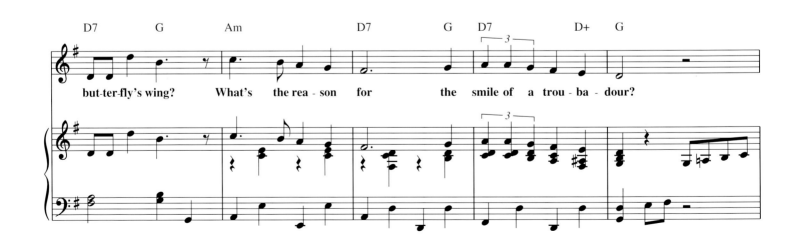

but-ter-fly's wing? What's the rea-son for the smile of a trou-ba-dour?

When You Wish Upon A Star

From Walt Disney's *Pinocchio*

Words by NED WASHINGTON
Music by LEIGH HARLINE

52

Baby Mine

From Walt Disney's *Dumbo*

Words by NED WASHINGTON
Music by FRANK CHURCHILL

Moderately slow

Ba - by mine _____ don't you cry. _____

Ba - by mine _____ dry your eye. _____

Rest your head close to my heart, nev - er to part, ba - by of

When I See An Elephant Fly

From Walt Disney's *Dumbo*

Words by NED WASHINGTON
Music by OLIVER WALLACE

Ho! Ho! When I think a-bout it, Ho! Ho! I have to laugh

Ho! Ho! Just to think a-bout it bends me right in half.

Little April Shower

From Walt Disney's *Bambi*

Words by LARRY MOREY
Music by FRANK CHURCHILL

Moderately

Drip, drip, drop, lit-tle A-pril show-er, beat-ing a tune as you
Drip, drip, drop, lit-tle A-pril show-er, beat-ing a tune ev-'ry-

fall all a-round. Drip, drip, drop, lit-tle A-pril show-er, what can com-pare with your
where that you fall. Drip, drip, drop, lit-tle A-pril show-er, I'm get-ting wet and I

beau-ti-ful sound. *To Coda* Drip, drip, drop, when the sky is cloud-y
don't care at all.

Zip-A-Dee-Doo-Dah

From Walt Disney's *Song Of The South*

Words by RAY GILBERT
Music by ALLIE WRUBEL

The Lord Is Good To Me

From Walt Disney's *Melody Time*

Words and Music by KIM GANNON
and WALTER KENT

Lyrics:

The Lord is good to me and so I thank the Lord for

giv-in' me the things I need the sun and rain and an ap-ple seed, yes

He's been good to me. *(whistle)*

68

Lavender Blue
(Dilly Dilly)
From Walt Disney's *So Dear To My Heart*

Words by LARRY MOREY
Music by ELIOT DANIEL

A Dream Is A Wish Your Heart Makes

From Walt Disney's *Cinderella*

Words and Music by MACK DAVID,
AL HOFFMAN and JERRY LIVINGSTON

Moderately slow, with expression

A dream is a wish your heart makes _____

when you're fast a - sleep. _____ In dreams you will

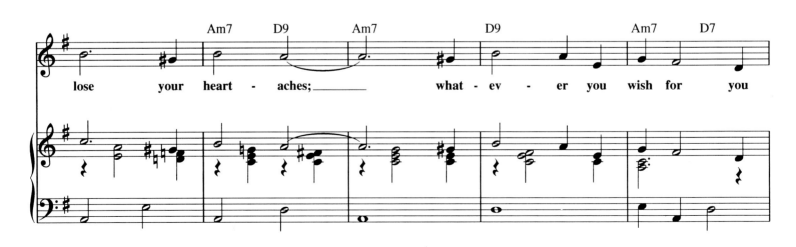

lose your heart - aches; _____ what - ev - er you wish for you

Bibbidi-Bobbidi-Boo
(The Magic Song)
From Walt Disney's *Cinderella*

Words by JERRY LIVINGSTON
Music by MACK DAVID and AL HOFFMAN

Salagadoola menchicka boola bibbidi-bobbidi-boo put 'em together and what have you got bibbidi-bobbidi-boo. Salagadoola menchicka boola bibbidi-bobbidi-boo

I'm Late

From Walt Disney's *Alice In Wonderland*

Words by BOB HILLIARD
Music by SAMMY FAIN

I'm late, I'm late for a ver-y im-por-tant date. No

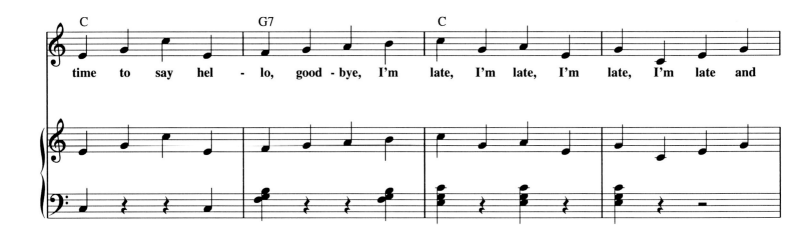

time to say hel - lo, good-bye, I'm late, I'm late, I'm late, I'm late and

when I wave, I lose the time I save. My fuz-zy ears and

78

The Second Star
To The Right

From Walt Disney's *Peter Pan*

Words by SAMMY CAHN
Music by SAMMY FAIN

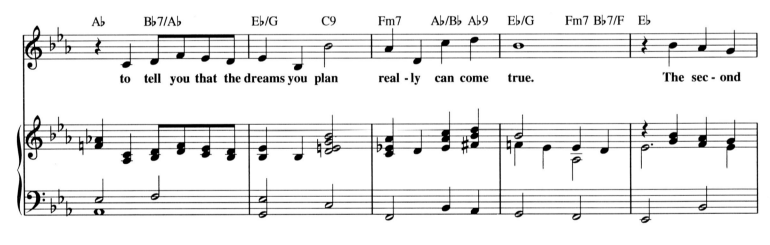

© 1951 Walt Disney Music Company
Copyright Renewed
All Rights Reserved   Used by Permission

You Can Fly!
You Can Fly! You Can Fly!

From Walt Disney's *Peter Pan*

Words by SAMMY CAHN
Music by SAMMY FAIN

Think of the pres-ents you're brought, an - y mer-ry lit - tle thought.

Think of Christ - mas, think of snow, think of sleigh bells, here we go! Like

rein-deer in the sky. _____ You can fly! You can

Soon you'll zoom all a - round the room, all it takes is faith and

trust. But the thing that's a pos - i - tive must is a lit - tle bit of Pix - ie

Dust. The dust is a pos - i - tive must! _____

When there's a smile in your heart there's no bet -ter time to start.

83

Bella Notte
(This Is The Night)

From Walt Disney's *Lady And The Tramp*

Words and Music by PEGGY LEE
and SONNY BURKE

Once Upon A Dream

From Walt Disney's *Sleeping Beauty*

Words and Music by SAMMY FAIN
and JACK LAWRENCE
Adapted From A Theme By Tchaikovsky

Cruella De Vil

From Walt Disney's *101 Dalmatians*

Words and Music by
MEL LEVEN

Cru - el - la De - Vil, __ Cru - el - la De - Vil, __ if she does-n't scare_ you no

ev - il thing will. __ To see her is to take a sud - den chill. _____ Cru-

el - la, Cru - el - la De - Vil. The curl of her lips, __ the

Higitus Figitus

From Walt Disney's *The Sword In The Stone*

Words and Music by RICHARD M. SHERMAN
and ROBERT B. SHERMAN

Lyrics under the music:

Hig - i - tus fig - i - tus zum - ba - ba - zing, I want your at - ten - tion ev - 'ry thing! We're

pack - ing to leave come on let's go, books are al - ways first you know.

Hock - e - ty pock - e - ty wock - e - ty wack, ab - ra - cab - ra dab - ra nack.

94

Shrink in size ver - y small, we've got to save e - nough room for all.

Hig - i - tus fig - i - tus mig - i - tus mum, pres - ti - dig - i - ton - i - um!

Ci - ce - ro you be - long to the "C's", al - pha - bet - i - cal

or - der please. Ali - i - ca - fez bal - a - ca - zez, mal - a - ca - mez mer - i - pi - des, di -

traf - fic jam. Sug - ar bowl you're get - ting rough, the poor old tea set's cracked e-nough.

Hock-et - y pock-et - y wock-et - y wack, odds and ends and bric a brac.

Hig - i - tus fig - i - tus mig - i - tus mum, pres - ti - dig - i - ton - i - um.

Hig - i - tus fig - i - tus mig - i - tus mum, pres - ti - dig - i - ton - i - um.

A Spoonful Of Sugar

From Walt Disney's *Mary Poppins*

Words and Music by RICHARD M. SHERMAN
and ROBERT B. SHERMAN

Supercalifragilistic-expialidocious

From Walt Disney's *Mary Poppins*

Words and Music by RICHARD M. SHERMAN
and ROBERT B. SHERMAN

Brightly

Mary Poppins:

Sup - er - cal - i - frag - il - is - tic - ex - pi - al - i - do - cious!

E - ven though the sound of it is some - thing quite a - tro - cious.

If you say it loud e - nough, you'll al - ways sound pre - co - cious.

The Bare Necessities

From Walt Disney's *The Jungle Book*

Words and Music by
TERRY GILKYSON

Trust In Me
(The Python's Song)
From Walt Disney's *The Jungle Book*

Words and Music by RICHARD M. SHERMAN
and ROBERT B. SHERMAN

Ev'rybody Wants To Be A Cat

From Walt Disney's *The Aristocats*

Words by FLOYD HUDDLESTON
Music by AL RINKER

Ev - 'ry-bod - y wants to be a cat, be-cause a cat's the on - ly cat who knows where it's at! __ Ev - 'ry-bod - y pick-in' up on the fe - line beat, __ 'cause ev - 'ry-thing else is ob - so - lete. Be - ware of a square __ when he of - fers to share __ his

The Age Of Not Believing

From Walt Disney's *Bedknobs And Broomsticks*

Words and Music by RICHARD M. SHERMAN
and ROBERT B. SHERMAN

When you rush a-round in hope-less cir-cles search-ing
set a-side your child-hood he-roes and your
face the age of not be-liev-ing, doubt-ing

ev-'ry-where for some-thing true. You're at the age of
dreams are lost up-on a shelf. You're at the age of
ev-'ry-thing you ev-er knew. Un-til at last you

not be-liev-ing when all the "make be-lieve" is
not be-liev-ing and worst of

Oo-De-Lally

From Walt Disney's *Robin Hood*

Words and Music by
ROGER MILLER

Moderately

Rob-in Hood and Lit-tle John walk-in' thru the for-est, laugh-in' back and forth at what the
Rob-in Hood and Lit-tle John run-nin' thru the for-est, jump-in' fen-ces dodg-in' trees and

oth-er 'un has to say. _____ Rem-i-nisc-in' this 'n that 'n
try-in' to get a-way. _____ Con-tem-plat-in' noth-in' but es-

hav-in' such a good time. / Oo-de-lal-ly, Hoo-de-lal-ly, gol-ly what a day! _____
cape and fin-'ly makin' it. \

Someone's Waiting For You

From Walt Disney's *The Rescuers*

Words by CAROL CONNORS and AYN ROBBINS
Music by SAMMY FAIN

Winnie The Pooh

From Walt Disney's
The Many Adventures Of Winnie The Pooh

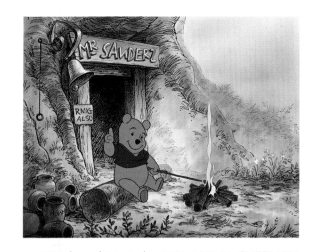

Words and Music by RICHARD M. SHERMAN
and ROBERT B. SHERMAN

Win - nie The Pooh, Win - nie The Pooh, tub - by lit - tle cub - by all stuffed with fluff. He's

Win - nie The Pooh, Win - nie The Pooh, wil - ly nil - ly sil - ly ole bear. _____ Deep in the

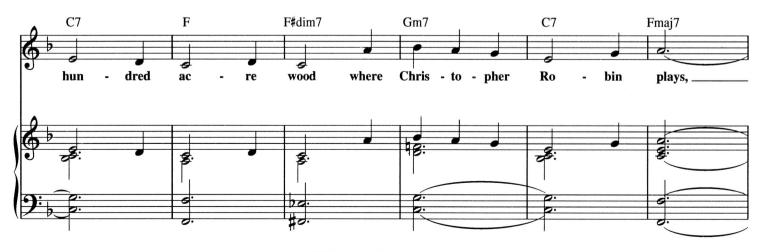

hun - dred ac - re wood where Chris - to - pher Ro - bin plays, _____

The Wonderful Thing About Tiggers

From Walt Disney's
The Many Adventures Of Winnie The Pooh

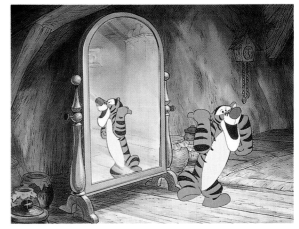

Words and Music by RICHARD M. SHERMAN
and ROBERT B. SHERMAN

Brightly

1., 3. The won-der-ful thing a-bout Tig - gers _____ is Tig-gers are won-der-ful
2. won-der-ful thing a-bout Tig - gers _____ is Tig-gers are won-der-ful

things! Their tops are made out of rub - ber; _____ their
chaps! They're load - ed with vim and with vig - or; _____ they

bot - toms are made out of springs! They're boun - cy, troun - cy, floun - cy, poun - cy,
love to leap in your laps! They're jump - y, bump - y, clump - y, thump - y,

123

Candle On The Water

From Walt Disney's *Pete's Dragon*

Words and Music by AL KASHA
and JOEL HIRSCHHORN

Lyrics:

I'll be your can-dle on the wa-ter, my love for you will al-ways burn. I know you're lost and drift-ing, but the clouds are lift-ing, don't give up you have some-where to turn.

I'll be your can-dle on the wa-ter, 'til ev-'ry wave is warm and bright, my soul is there be-side you, let this can-dle guide you soon you'll see a gold-en stream of light.

Best Of Friends

From Walt Disney's *The Fox And The Hound*

Words by STAN FIDEL
Music by RICHARD JOHNSTON

When you're the best of friends _____ hav-ing so much fun to-geth-
hap-py game, _____ you could clown a-round for-ev-

-er, you're not e-ven a-ware __ you're such a fun-ny pair. __
-er. Nei-ther one of you sees __ your nat-ur'l bound-a-ries. __

1 You're the best _ of friends. _ Life's a
2 Life's one hap-py game.

Perfect Isn't Easy

From Walt Disney's *Oliver & Company*

Words by JACK FELDMAN
and BRUCE SUSSMAN
Music by BARRY MANILOW

Moderately

Girls, we've got work to do. ___ Pass me the paint and glue.

Per - fect is - n't eas - y but it's me. _____ When one knows the

world is watch - ing, one does what one must. Some mi - nor ad - just - ments, dar - ling;

Kiss The Girl

From Walt Disney's *The Little Mermaid*

Lyrics by HOWARD ASHMAN
Music by ALAN MENKEN

Kiss The Girl

From Walt Disney's *The Little Mermaid*

Lyrics by Howard Ashman
Music by Alan Menken

There you see her sitting there across the way.
She don't got a lot to say, but there's something about her.
And you don't know why, but you're dying to try.
You wanna kiss the girl.
Yes, you want her.
Look at her, you know you do.
Possible she wants you, too.
There is one way to ask her.
It don't take a word, not a single word, go on and kiss the girl.
Sha la la la la la, my oh my,
Look like the boy too shy.
Ain't gonna kiss the girl.
Sha la la la la la, ain't that sad.
Ain't it a shame, too bad.
He gonna miss the girl.
Now's your moment, floating in a blue lagoon.
Boy, you better do it soon, no time will be better.
She don't say a word and she won't say a word until you kiss the girl.
Sha la la la la la, don't be scared.
You got the mood prepared, go on and kiss the girl.
Sha la la la la la, don't stop now.
Don't try to hide it how
You wanna kiss the girl. Sha la la la la la, float along.
And listen to the song, the song say kiss the girl.
Sha la la la la the music play.
Do what the music say.
You gotta kiss the girl.
You've got to kiss the girl.
You wanna kiss the girl.
You've gotta kiss the girl.
Go on and kiss the girl.

Under The Sea

From Walt Disney's *The Little Mermaid*

Lyrics by HOWARD ASHMAN
Music by ALAN MENKEN

Under The Sea

From Walt Disney's *The Little Mermaid*

Lyrics by Howard Ashman
Music by Alan Menken

The seaweed is always greener in somebody else's lake.
You dream about going up there.
But that is a big mistake.
Just look at the world around you, right here on the ocean floor.
Such wonderful things surround you.
What more is you lookin' for?
Under the sea, under the sea.
Darlin' it's better down where it's wetter.
Take it from me.
Up on the shore they work all day.
Out in the sun they slave away.
While we devotin' full time to floatin' under the sea.
Down here all the fish is happy as off through the waves they roll.
The fish on the land ain't happy.
They sad 'cause they in the bowl.
But fish in the bowl is lucky, they in for a worser fate.
One day when the boss get hungry guess who gon' be on the plate.
Under the sea, under the sea.
Nobody beat us, fry us and eat us in fricassee.
We what the land folks loves to cook.
Under the sea we off the hook.
We got no troubles life is the bubbles under the sea.
Under the sea.
Since life is sweet here we got the beat here naturally.
Even the sturgeon an' the ray they get the urge 'n' start to play.
We got the spirit, you got to hear it under the sea.
The newt play the flute.
The carp play the harp.
The plaice play the bass.
And they soundin' sharp.
The bass play the brass.
The chub play the tub.
The fluke is the duke of soul.
The ray he can play.
The lings on the strings.
The trout rockin' out.
The blackfish she sings.
The smelt and the sprat they know where it's at.
An' oh, that blowfish blow.
Under the sea.
Under the sea.
When the sardine begin the beguine it's music to me.
What do they got, a lot of sand.
We got a hot crustacean band.
Each little clam here know how to jam here under the sea.
Each little slug here cuttin'a rug here under the sea.
Each little snail here know how to wail here.
That's why it's hotter under the water.
Ya we in luck here down in the muck here under the sea.

Part Of Your World

From Walt Disney's *The Little Mermaid*

Lyrics by HOWARD ASHMAN
Music by ALAN MENKEN

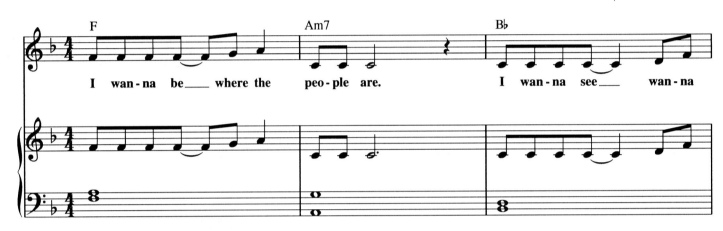

I wan-na be___ where the peo-ple are. I wan-na see___ wan-na

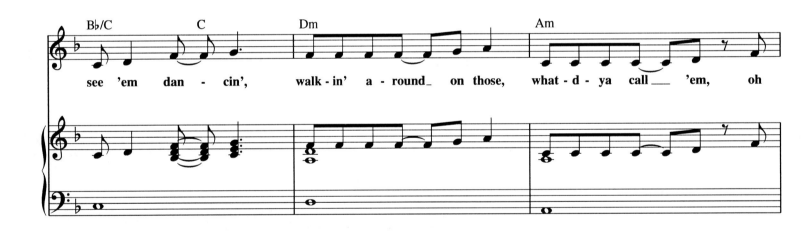

see 'em dan - cin', walk-in' a - round___ on those, what-d-ya call___ 'em, oh

feet. Flip-pin' your fins___ you don't get too far.___

Part Of Your World

From Walt Disney's *The Little Mermaid*

Lyrics by Howard Ashman
Music by Alan Menken

Look at this stuff.

Isn't it neat?

Wouldn't you think my collection's complete?

Wouldn't you think I'm the girl, the girl who has ev'rything.

Look at this trove, treasures untold.

How many wonders can one cavern hold?

Looking around here you'd think, sure, she's got ev'rything.

I've got gadgets and gizmos aplenty.

I've got whozits and whatzits galore.

You want thingamabobs, I've got twenty.

But who cares?

No big deal. I want more.

I wanna be where the people are.

I wanna see wanna see 'em dancin',

Walkin' around on those, whatdya call 'em, oh feet.

Flippin' your fins you don't get too far.

Legs are required for jumpin', dancin'.

Strollin' along down the, what's that word again, street.

Up where they walk, up where they run, up where they stay all day in the sun.

Wanderin' free, wish I could be part of that world.

What would I give if I could live outta these waters.

What would I pay to spend a day warm on the sand.

Betcha on land they understand.

Bet they don't reprimand their daughters.

Bright young women, sick of swimmin', ready to stand.

And ready to know what the people know.

Ask 'em my questions and get some answers.

What's a fire and why does it, what's the word, burn.

When's it my turn?

Wouldn't I love, love to explore that shore up above, out of the sea.

Wish I could be part of that world.

Beauty And The Beast

From Walt Disney's *Beauty And The Beast*

Lyrics by HOWARD ASHMAN
Music by ALAN MENKEN

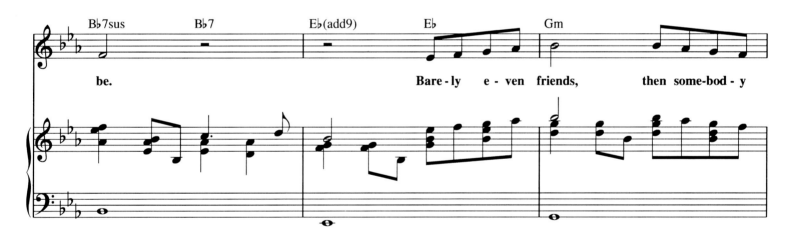

152

Beauty And The Beast

From Walt Disney's *Beauty And The Beast*

Lyrics by Howard Ashman
Music by Alan Menken

Tale as old as time,
True as it can be.
Barely even friends,
Then somebody bends
Unexpectedly.
Just a little change.
Small to say the least.
Both a little scared,
Neither one prepared.
Beauty and the Beast.
Ever just the same.
Ever a surprise.
Ever as before,
Ever just as sure
As the sun will rise.
Tale as old as time.
Tune as old as song.
Bittersweet and strange,
Finding you can change,
Learning you were wrong.
Certain as the sun
Rising in the East.
Tale as old as time,
Song as old as rhyme.
Beauty and the Beast.
Tale as old as time,
Song as old as rhyme.
Beauty and the Beast.

Be Our Guest

From Walt Disney's *Beauty And The Beast*

Lyrics by HOWARD ASHMAN
Music by ALAN MENKEN

Be our guest! Be our guest! Put our ser - vice to the

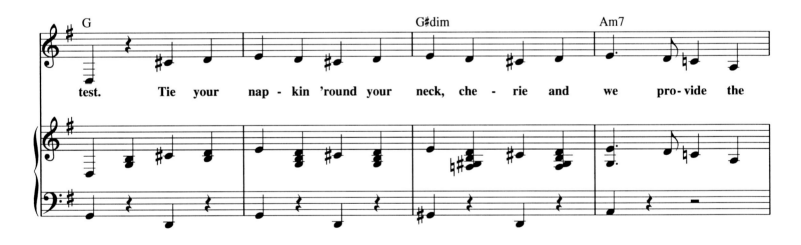

test. Tie your nap - kin 'round your neck, che - rie and we pro- vide the

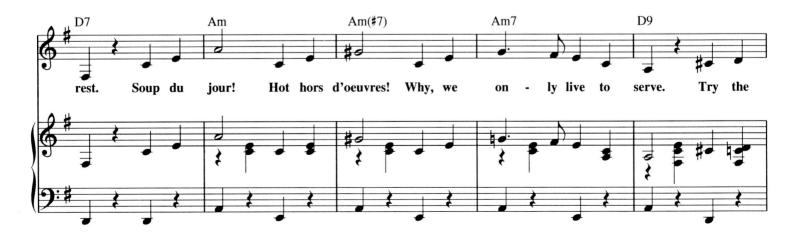

rest. Soup du jour! Hot hors d'oeuvres! Why, we on - ly live to serve. Try the

Be Our Guest

From Walt Disney's *Beauty And The Beast*

Lyrics by Howard Ashman
Music by Alan Menken

Lumiere:	Ma chere Mademoiselle, It is with deepest pride and greatest pleasure that we welcome you tonight. And now, we invite you to relax. Let us pull up a chair as the dining room proudly presents your dinner!
	Be our guest! Be our guest! Put our service to the test.
	Tie your napkin 'round your neck, cherie, And we provide the rest. Soup du jour! Hot hors d'oeuvres!
	Why, we only live to serve. Try the grey stuff, it's delicious! Don't believe me? Ask the dishes!
	They can sing! They can dance! After all, Miss, this is France! And a dinner here is never second best.
	Go on, unfold your menu, Take a glance, And then you'll be our guest, Oui, our guest! Be our guest!
	Beef ragout! Cheese souffle! Pie and pudding "en flambe!" We'll prepare and serve with flair A culinary cabaret!
	You're alone and you're scared But the banquet's all prepared. No one's gloomy or complaining While the flatware's entertaining.
	We tell jokes. I do tricks with my fellow candlesticks.
Mugs:	And it's all in perfect taste. That you can bet!
All:	Come on and lift your glass You've won your own free pass To be our guest!
Lumeniere:	If you're stressed, It's fine dining we suggest.
All:	Be our guest! Be our guest! Be our guest!
Lumeniere:	Life is so unnerving for a servant who's not serving. He's not whole without a soul to wait upon. Ah, those good old days when we were useful. Suddenly, those good old days are gone.

Ten years, we've been rusting,
Needing so much more — than dusting.
Needing exercise, a chance to use our skills.

Most days, we just lay around the castle.
Flabby, fat and lazy.
You walked in and oops-a-daisy.

Mrs. Potts: It's a guest!
It's a guest!
Sakes alive,
Well, I'll be blessed!

Wine's been poured and thank the Lord
I've had the napkins freshly pressed.
With dessert she'll want tea.

And my dear, that's fine with me.
While the cups do their soft shoeing,
I'll be bubbling!
I'll be brewing!

I'll get warm, piping hot!
Heaven's sakes!
Is that a spot?
Clean it up!

We want the company impressed!
We've got a lot to do.
Is it one lump or two
For you, our guest?

Chorus: She's our guest!

Mrs. Potts: She's our guest!

Chorus: She's our guest!
Be our guest!
Be our guest!

Our command is your request.
It's ten years since we had anybody here,
And we're obsessed.

With your meal
With your ease,
Yes, indeed,
We aim to please.

While the candlelight's still glowing
Let us help you,
We'll keep going.

Course by course,
One by one!
'Til you shout,
"Enough. I'm done!"

Then we'll sing you off to sleep as you digest.
Tonight you'll prop your feet up!
But for now, let's eat up!

Be our guest!
Be our guest!
Be our guest!
Please, be our guest!

Belle

From Walt Disney's *Beauty And The Beast*

Lyrics by HOWARD ASHMAN
Music by ALAN MENKEN

Moderately fast

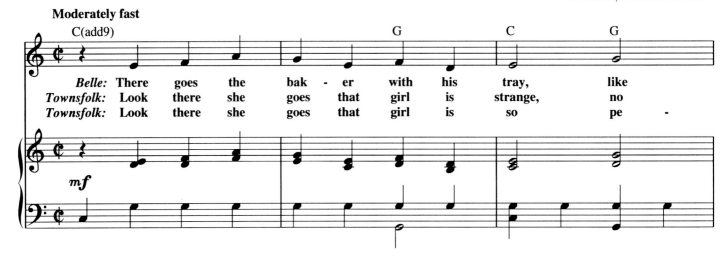

Belle: There goes the bak - er with his tray, like
Townsfolk: Look there she goes that girl is strange, no
Townsfolk: Look there she goes that girl is so pe -

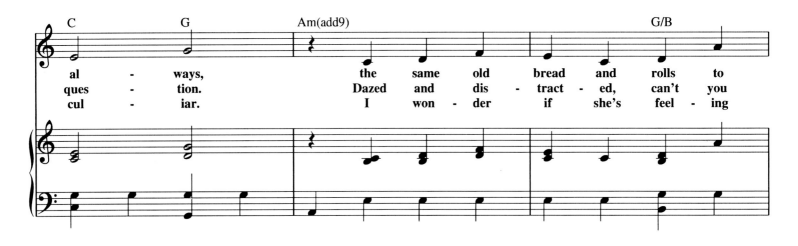

al - ways, the same old bread and rolls to
ques - tion. Dazed and dis - tract - ed, can't you
cul - iar. I won - der if she's feel - ing

sell. Ev -'ry morn - ing just the
tell? Nev - er part of an - y
well. With a dream - y, far - off

Belle

From Walt Disney's *Beauty And The Beast*

Lyrics by Howard Ashman
Music by Alan Menken

Belle:	Little town, it's a quiet village. Ev'ry day like the one before. Little town full of little people Waking up to say:
Townsfolk:	Bonjour! Bonjour! Bonjour! Bonjour! Bonjour!
Belle:	There goes the baker with his tray, like always, The same old bread and rolls to sell. Ev'ry morning just the same Since the morning that we came To this poor provincial town.
Baker:	Good Morning, Belle!
Belle:	Morning, Monsieur.
Baker:	Where are you off to?
Belle:	The bookshop. I just finished the most wonderful story about a beanstalk and an ogre and a...
Baker:	That's nice. Marie! The baguettes! Hurry up!
Townsfolk:	Look there she goes that girl is strange, no question. Dazed and distracted, can't you tell? Never part of any crowd, 'Cause her head's up on some cloud. No denying she's a funny girl, that Belle.
Man I:	Bonjour.
Woman I:	Good day.
Man I:	How is your fam'ly?
Woman II:	Bonjour.
Man II:	Good day.
Woman II:	How is your wife?
Woman III:	I need six eggs!
Man III:	That's too expensive.
Belle:	There must be more than this provincial life.
Bookseller:	Ah, Belle!
Belle:	Good morning. I've come to return the book I borrowed.
Bookseller:	Finished already?
Belle:	Oh, I couldn't put it down. Have you got anything new?
Bookseller:	Ha, ha! Not since yesterday.
Belle:	That's alright. I'll borrow this one!
Bookseller:	That one? But you've read it twice!
Belle:	Well, it's my favorite! Far off places, daring sword fights, Magic spells, a prince in disguise...

Bookseller:	If you like it all that much, it's yours!
Belle:	But sir!
Bookseller:	I insist.
Belle:	Well, thank you. Thank you very much!
Townsfolk:	Look there she goes that girl is so peculiar. I wonder if she's feeling well. With a dreamy, far-off look And her nose stuck in a book, What a puzzle to the rest of us is Belle.
Belle:	Oh, isn't this amazing? It's my fav'rite part because you'll see. Here's where she meets Prince Charming But she won't discover that it's him 'til chapter three.
Woman:	Now, it's no wonder that her name means "beauty." Her looks have got no parallel.
Shopkeeper:	But behind that fair facade. I'm afraid she's rather odd. Very diff'rent from the rest of us.
Townsfolk:	She's nothing like the rest of us. Yes, diff'rent from the rest of us is Belle.
Gaston:	Right from the moment when I met her, saw her, I said she's gorgeous and I fell. Here in town there's only she who is beautiful as me, I'm making plans to woo and marry Belle.
Silly Girls:	Look there he goes! Isn't he dreamy? Monsieur Gaston! Oh, he's so cute! Be still my heart! I'm hardly breathing! He's such a tall, dark, strong and handsome brute.
Man I:	Bonjour!
Man II:	Good day.
Matron:	You call this bacon?
Man IV:	Some cheese... ...One pound.
Cheese Merchant:	I'll get the knife.
Woman I:	This bread... ...It's stale!
Baker:	Madame's mistaken.
Belle:	There must be more than this provincial life!
Gaston:	Just watch I'm going to make Belle my wife!
Townsfolk:	Look there she goes a girl who's strange but special. A most peculiar mad'moiselle. It's a pity and a sin. She doesn't quite fit in 'Cause she really is a funny girl A beauty but a funny girl. She really is a funny girl That Belle!

Friend Like Me

From Walt Disney's *Aladdin*

Lyrics by HOWARD ASHMAN
Music by ALAN MENKEN

Friend Like Me

From Walt Disney's *Aladdin*

Lyrics by Howard Ashman
Music by Alan Menken

Genie: Well, Ali Baba had them forty thieves.
Scheherazade had a thousand tales.
But, master, you in luck 'cause up your sleeves
You got a brand of magic never fails.
You got some power in your corner now,
Some heavy ammunition in your camp.
You got some punch, pizazz, yahoo and how.
See, all you gotta do is rub that lamp.
And I'll say, Mister Aladdin, sir,
What will your pleasure be?
Let me take your order, jot it down.
You ain't never had a friend like me. No no no.
Life is your restaurant and I'm your maitre d'.
C'mon whisper what it is you want.
You ain't never had a friend like me.
Yes sir, we pride ourselves on service.
You're the boss, the king, the shah.
Say what you wish. It's yours!
True dish, how 'bout a little more baklava?
Have some of column "A".
Try all of column "B".
I'm in the mood to help you, dude,
You ain't never had a friend like me.
Wa-ah-ah. Oh my.
Wa-ah-ah. No no.
Wah-ah-ah. Na na na.
Can your friends do this?
Can your friends do that?
Can your friends pull this out their little hat?
Can your friends go poof!
(Spoken:) *Well, looky here.*
Can your friends go abracadabra,
Let 'er rip and then make the sucker disappear?
So doncha sit there slack jawed, buggy eyed.
I'm here to answer all your midday prayers.
You got me bonafide certified.
You got a genie for your chargé d'affaires.
I got a powerful urge to help you out.
So whatcha wish I really want to know.
You got a list that's three miles long, no doubt.
Well, all you gotta do is rub like so. And oh.
Mister Aladdin, sir, have a wish or two or three.
I'm on the job, you big nabob.
You ain't never had a friend, never had a friend,
You ain't never had a friend, never had a friend.
You ain't never had a friend like me.
Wa-ah-ah. Wa-ah-ah.
You ain't never had a friend like me. Ha!

A Whole New World

From Walt Disney's *Aladdin*

Music by ALAN MENKEN
Lyrics by TIM RICE

A Whole New World
From Walt Disney's *Aladdin*

Music by Alan Menken
Lyrics by Tim Rice

Aladdin:	I can show you the world,
	Shining, shimmering, splendid.
	Tell me princess, now
	When did you last let your heart decide?
	I can open your eyes
	Take you wonder by wonder
	Over, sideways and under on a magic carpet ride.
	A whole new world,
	A new fantastic point of view.
	No one to tell us no or where to go
	Or say we're only dreaming.
Jasmine:	A whole new world,
	A dazzling place I never knew.
	But when I'm way up here it's crystal clear
	That now I'm in a whole new world with you.
Aladdin:	Now I'm in a whole new world with you.
Jasmine:	Unbelievable sights, indescribable feeling.
	Soaring, tumbling, free-wheeling
	Through an endless diamond sky.
	A whole new world,
Aladdin:	Don't you dare close your eyes.
Jasmine:	A hundred thousand things to see.
Aladdin:	Hold your breath, it gets better.
Jasmine:	I'm like a shooting star I've come so far
	I can't go back to where I used to be.
Aladdin:	A whole new world.
Jasmine:	Every turn a surprise.
Aladdin:	With new horizons to pursue.
Jasmine:	Ev'ry moment red-letter.
Both:	I'll chase them anywhere. There's time to spare.
	Let me share this whole new world with you.
Aladdin:	A whole new world,
Jasmine:	A whole new world,
Aladdin:	That's where we'll be.
Jasmine:	That's where we'll be.
Aladdin:	A thrilling chase
Jasmine:	A wond'rous place
Both:	For you and me.

174

One Jump Ahead

From Walt Disney's *Aladdin*

Music by ALAN MENKEN
Lyrics by TIM RICE

Gotta keep one jump a-head of the bread-line, one swing a-

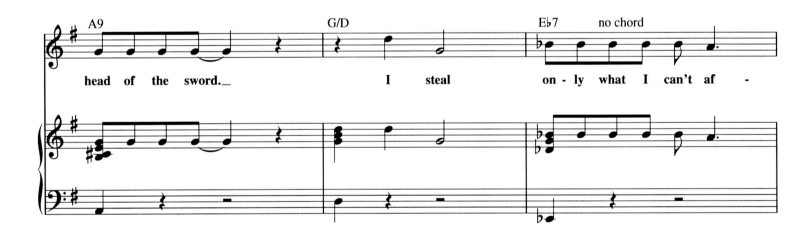

head of the sword.___ I steal on-ly what I can't af-

ford. That's ev-'ry-thing! One jump a-

One Jump Ahead

From Walt Disney's *Aladdin*

Music by Alan Menken
Lyrics by Tim Rice

Aladdin:	Gotta keep one jump ahead of the breadline,
	One swing ahead of the sword.
	I steal only what I can't afford.
	(Spoken:) *That's everything!*
	One jump ahead of the lawmen.
	That's all, and that's no joke.
	These guys don't appreciate I'm broke.
Crowd:	Riff raff! Street rat! Scoundrel! Take that!
Aladdin:	Just a little snack, guys.
Crowd:	Rip him open, take it back, guys.
Aladdin:	I can take a hint, gotta face the facts.
	You're my only friend, Abu!
Crowd:	Who?
Ladies:	Oh it's sad Aladdin's hit the bottom.
	He's become a one man rise in crime.
	I'd blame parents except he hasn't got 'em.
Aladdin:	Gotta eat to live, gotta steal to eat,
	Tell you all about it when I got the time!
	One jump ahead of the slowpokes,
	One skip ahead of my doom.
	Next time gonna use a nom-de-plume.
	One jump ahead of the hitmen,
	One hit ahead of the flock.
	I think I'll take a stroll around the block.
Crowd:	Stop thief! Vandal! Outrage! Scandal!
Aladdin:	Let's not be too hasty.
Lady:	Still I think he's rather tasty.
Aladdin:	Gotta eat to live, gotta steal to eat,
	Otherwise we'd get along.
Crowd:	(Spoken:) *Wrong!*
Aladdin:	One jump ahead of the hoofbeats.
Crowd:	Vandal!
Aladdin:	One hop ahead of the hump.
Crowd:	Streetrat!
Aladdin:	One trick ahead of disaster.
Crowd:	Scoundrel!
Aladdin:	They're quick but I'm much faster.
Crowd:	Take that!
Aladdin:	Here goes. Better throw my hand in.
	Wish me happy landin'.
	All I gotta do is jump!

Circle Of Life

From Walt Disney Pictures' *The Lion King*

Music by ELTON JOHN
Lyrics by TIM RICE

Relaxed Pop beat

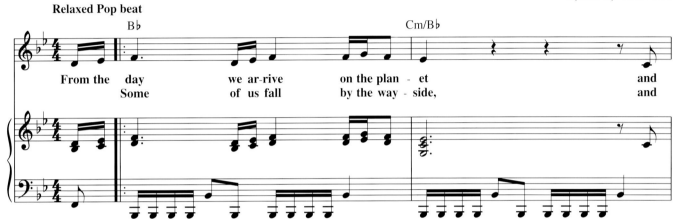

From the day / Some

we ar-rive / of us fall

on the plan - et / by the way - side,

and / and

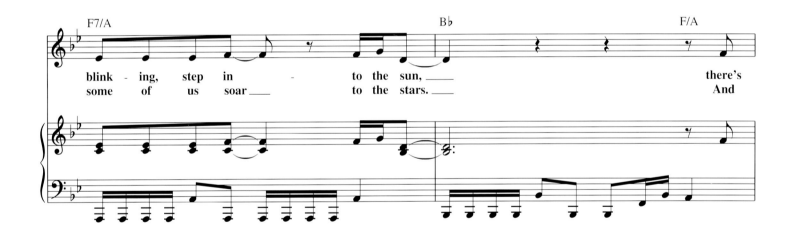

blink - ing, / some of us soar

step in - / to the sun, / to the stars.

there's / And

more to be seen / some of us sail

than can ev - er be seen, / through our trou - bles,

more to do / and some

184

Can You Feel The Love Tonight

From Walt Disney Pictures' *The Lion King*

Music by ELTON JOHN
Lyrics by TIM RICE

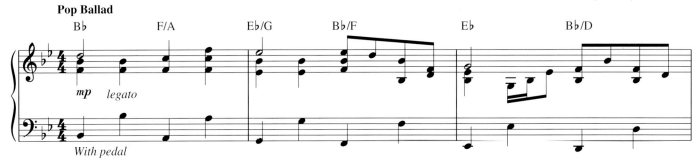

There's a calm_ sur-ren - der to the rush_ of day,__
There's a time_ for ev'ry-one, if they on - ly learn_

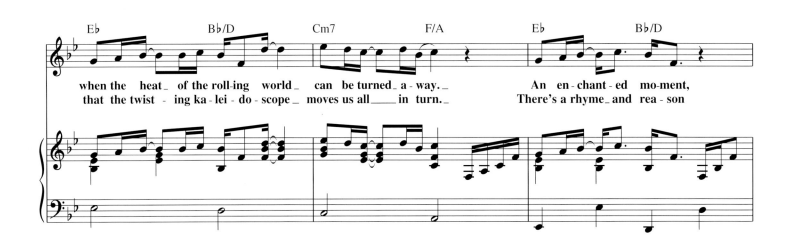

when the heat_ of the roll-ing world_ can be turned_ a - way.__
that the twist - ing ka - lei - do - scope_ moves us all____ in turn.__

An en - chant - ed mo-ment,
There's a rhyme_ and rea - son

Hakuna Matata

From Walt Disney Pictures' *The Lion King*

Music by ELTON JOHN
Lyrics by TIM RICE

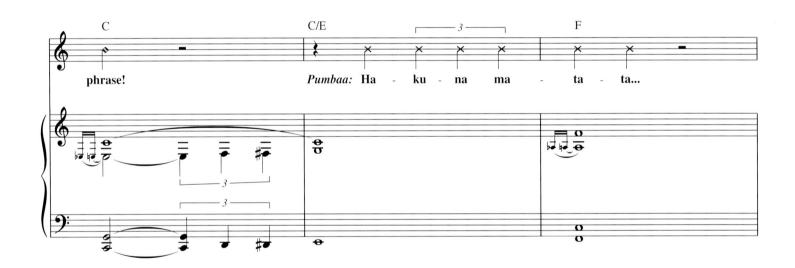

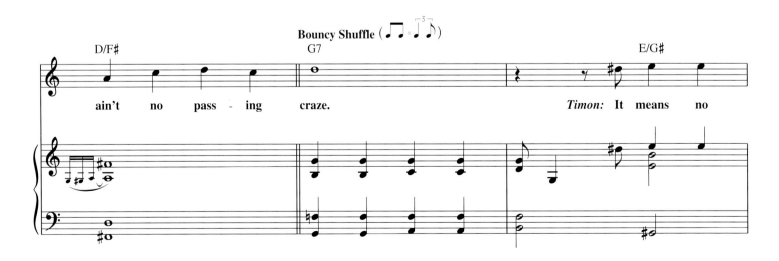

Hakuna Matata

From Walt Disney Pictures' *The Lion King*

Music by Elton John
Lyrics by Tim Rice

Timon:	Hakuna matata...what a wonderful phrase!
Pumbaa:	Hakuna matata...ain't no passing craze.
Timon:	It means no worries for the rest of your days.
Timon & Pumbaa:	It's our problem-free philosophy.
Timon:	Hakuna matata.
	Why, when he was a young warthog...
Pumbaa:	When I was a young warthog!
Timon:	(Spoken:) *Very nice.*
Pumbaa:	(Spoken:) *Thanks.*
Timon:	He found his aroma lacked a certain appeal.
	He could clear the savannah after ev'ry meal!
Pumbaa:	I'm a sensitive soul, though I seem thick-skinned.
	And it hurt that my friends never stood downwind!
	And, oh, the shame!
Timon:	He was ashamed!
Pumbaa:	Thought of changin' my name!
Timon:	Oh, what's in a name?
Pumbaa:	And I got downhearted...
Timon:	How did you feel?
Pumbaa:	...ev'ry time that I...
Timon:	(Spoken:) *Hey, Pumbaa, not in front of the kids.*
Pumbaa:	(Spoken:) *Oh, sorry.*
Timon & Pumbaa:	Hakuna matata...what a wonderful phrase.
	Hakuna matata...ain't no passing craze.
Simba:	It means no worries for the rest of your days.
Timon:	(Spoken:) *Yeah, sing it kid!*
Timon & Simba:	It's our problem-free
Pumbaa:	Philosophy.
Timon & Simba:	Hakuna matata.
All:	Hakuna matata. Hakuna matata. Hakuna matata.
	Hakuna matata. Hakuna matata. Hakuna matata.
	Hakuna matata. Hakuna...
Timon:	It means no worries for the rest of your days.
All:	It's our problem-free philosophy.
Timon:	Hakuna matata.
Pumbaa:	Hakuna matata. Hakuna matata.
Timon:	Hakuna matata.
Pumbaa:	Hakuna matata. Hakuna matata.
Timon:	Hakuna matata. Hakuna matata.
	Hakuna matata. Hakuna matata.

Colors Of The Wind

From Walt Disney's *Pocahontas*

Music by ALAN MENKEN
Lyrics by STEPHEN SCHWARTZ

198

If I Never Knew You
(Love Theme from POCAHONTAS)

From Walt Disney's *Pocahontas*

Music by ALAN MENKEN
Lyrics by STEPHEN SCHWARTZ

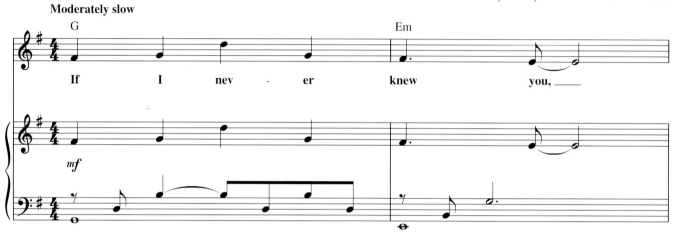

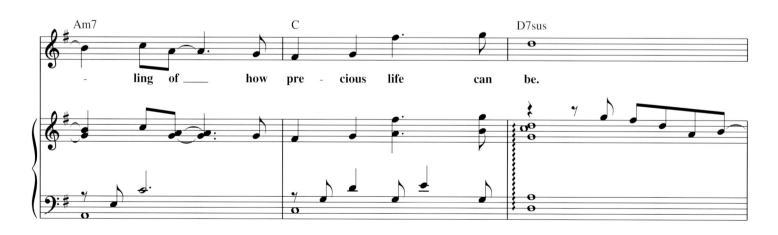

If I Never Knew You

(Love Theme from POCAHONTAS)
From Walt Disney's *Pocahontas*

Music by Alan Menken
Lyrics by Stephen Schwartz

Male:	If I never knew you, if I never felt this love,
	I would have no inkling of how precious life can be.
	And if I never held you, I would never have a clue
	How, at last, I'd find in you the missing part of me.
	In this world so full of fear, full of rage and lies,
	I can see the truth so clear in your eyes,
	So dry your eyes.
	And I'm so grateful to you.
	I'd have lived my whole life through,
	Lost forever if I never knew you.
Female:	If I never knew you, I'd be safe but half as real,
	Never knowing I could feel a love so strong and true.
	I'm so grateful to you.
	I'd have lived my whole life through,
	Lost forever if I never knew you.
Male:	I thought our love would be so beautiful.
Female:	Somehow we'd make the whole world bright.
Both:	I never knew that fear and hate could be so strong,
	All they'd leave us were these whispers in the night,
	But still my heart is saying we were right.
Female:	Oh. If I never knew you,
Male:	There's no moment I regret
Female:	If I never knew this love,
Male:	Since the moment that we met.
Female:	I would have no inkling of how precious life can be.
Male:	If our time has gone too fast I've lived at last.
Both:	I thought our love would be so beautiful,
	Somehow we'd make the whole world bright.
Female:	I thought our love would be so beautiful,
	We'd turn the darkness into light.
Both:	And still my heart is saying we were right.
Male:	We were right. And if I never knew you,
Female:	If I never knew you,
Male:	I'd have lived my whole life through
Female:	Empty as the sky,
Both:	Never knowing why,
	Lost forever if I never knew you.

You've Got A Friend In Me

From Walt Disney's *Toy Story*

Music and Lyrics by
RANDY NEWMAN

Lyrics:

You've got a friend in me.
You've got a friend in me.

You've got a friend in me.
You've got a friend in me.

When the road looks rough ahead and you're miles
You got troubles, then I got 'em too.

Someday

From Walt Disney's *The Hunchback Of Notre Dame*

Music by ALAN MENKEN
Lyrics by STEPHEN SCHWARTZ

Some-day when we are wis-er, when the world's old-er, when we have

learned. I pray some-day we may yet live to

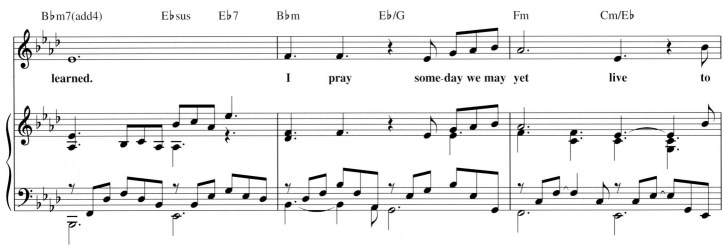

God Help The Outcasts

From Walt Disney's *The Hunchback Of Notre Dame*

Music by ALAN MENKEN
Lyrics by STEPHEN SCHWARTZ

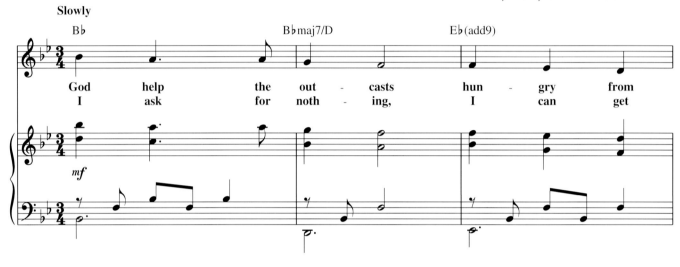

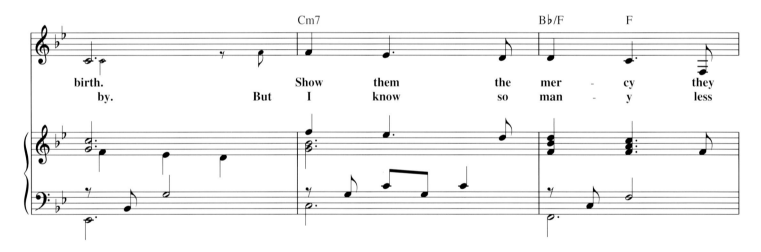

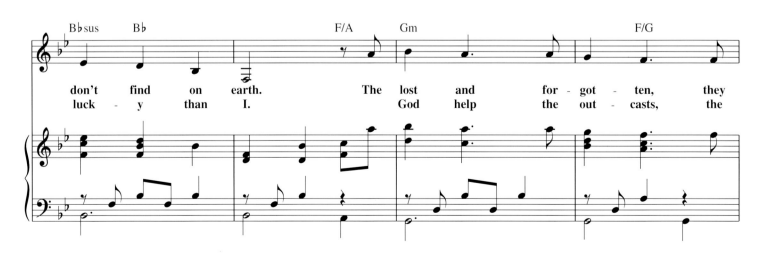

214

God Help The Outcasts

(As Performed by Bette Midler)
From Walt Disney's *The Hunchback Of Notre Dame*

Music by Alan Menken
Lyrics by Stephen Schwartz

I don't know if You can hear me or if You're even there.
I don't know if You will listen to a humble prayer.
They tell me I am just an outcast;
I shouldn't speak to You.
Still I see Your face and wonder:
Were You once an outcast too?
God help the outcasts hungry from birth.
Show them the mercy they don't find on earth.
The lost and forgotten, they look to You still.
God help the outcasts or nobody will.
I ask for nothing, I can get by.
But I know so many less lucky than I.
God help the outcasts, the poor and downtrod.
I thought we all were the children of God.
I don't know if there's a reason why some are blessed, some not.
Why the few You seem to favor, they fear us,
Flee us, try not to see us.
God help the outcasts, the tattered, the torn,
Seeking an answer to why they were born.
Winds of misfortune have blown them about.
You made the outcasts; don't cast them out.
The poor and unlucky, the weak and the odd;
I thought we all were the children of God.

Go The Distance

From Walt Disney Pictures' *Hercules*

Music by ALAN MENKEN
Lyrics by DAVID ZIPPEL

218

Go The Distance

(As Performed by Michael Bolton)
From Walt Disney Pictures' *Hercules*

Music by Alan Menken
Lyrics by David Zippel

I have often dreamed of a far-off place
Where a hero's welcome would be waiting for me,
Where the crowds will cheer when they see my face,
And a voice keeps saying this is where I'm meant to be.
I'll be there someday.
I can go the distance.
I will find my way if I can be strong.
I know ev'ry mile will be worth my while.
When I go the distance, I'll be right where I belong.
Down an unknown road to embrace my fate,
Though that road may wander it will lead me to you.
And a thousand years would be worth the wait.
It might take a lifetime, but somehow I'll see it through.
And I won't look back.
I can go the distance.
And I'll stay on track.
No, I won't accept defeat.
It's an uphill slope, but I won't lose hope
Till I go the distance and my journey is complete.
Oh, yeah.
But to look beyond the glory is the hardest part,
For a hero's strength is measured by his heart.
Like a shooting star, I will go the distance.
I will search the world.
I will face its harms.
I don't care how far.
I can go the distance
Till I find my hero's welcome waiting in your arms.
I will search the world.
I will face its harms
Till I find my hero's welcome waiting in your arms.

Zero To Hero

From Walt Disney Pictures' *Hercules*

Music by ALAN MENKEN
Lyrics by DAVID ZIPPEL

Driving 4

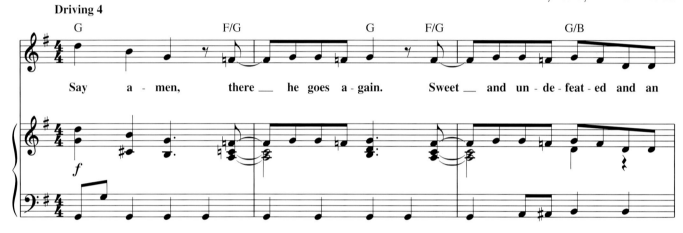

Say a - men, there __ he goes a - gain. Sweet __ and un - de - feat - ed and an

awe - some ten for ten. __ Folks lined up just __ to watch him flex, and __ this per - fect pack - age packed a

pair of per - fect pecs. Herc - ie, he comes, __ he sees, __ he con - quers. Hon - ey, the crowds __ were go -

224

225

Zero To Hero

From Walt Disney Pictures' *Hercules*

Music by Alan Menken
Lyrics by David Zippel

Muses: Bless my soul, Herc was on a roll.
Person of the week in ev'ry Greek opinion poll.
What a pro, Herc could stop a show.
Point him at a monster and you're talkin' S.R.O.
He was a no one, a zero, zero.
Now he's a honcho, he's a hero.
Here was a kid with his act down pat.
From zero to hero in no time flat.
Zero to hero, just like that.
When he smiled the girls went wild with oohs and ahs.
And they slapped his face on ev'ry vase.
On ev'ry vahse.
From appearance fees and royalties our Herc had cash to burn.
Now nouveau riche and famous he could tell you
What's a Grecian urn.
Say amen there he goes again.
Sweet and undefeated and an awesome ten for ten.
Folks lined up just to watch him flex.
And this perfect package packed a pair of perfect pecs.
Hercie, he comes, he sees, he conquers.
Honey, the crowds were going bonkers.
He showed the moxie, brains and spunk.
From zero to hero, a major hunk.
Zero to hero (Spoken:) *and who'd athunk?*
Who put the glad in gladiator? Hercules.
Whose daring deeds are great theater? Hercules.
Is he bold? No one braver.
Is he sweet? Our fav'rite flavor. Hercules.
Hercules. Hercules. Hercules. Hercules. Hercules.
Bless my soul, Herc was on a roll, undefeated.
Riding high (Spoken:) *and the nicest guy.*
Not conceited. He was a nothing, zero, zero.
Now he's a honcho, he's a hero.
He hit the heights at breakneck speed.
From zero to hero. Herc is a hero.
Now he's a hero. (Spoken:) *Yes, indeed.*

Honor To Us All

From Walt Disney Pictures' *Mulan*

Music by MATTHEW WILDER
Lyrics by DAVID ZIPPEL

Very quickly, in 2

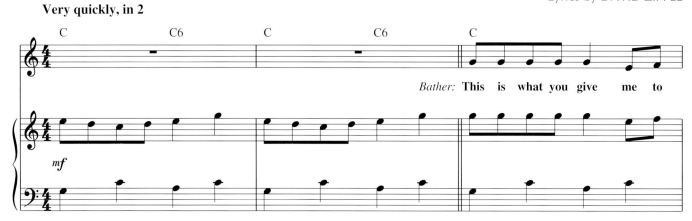

Bather: This is what you give me to

work with. Well, hon-ey, I've seen worse.

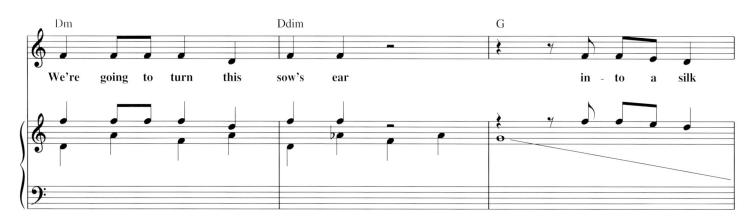

We're going to turn this sow's ear in-to a silk

purse.

We'll have you washed and dried,

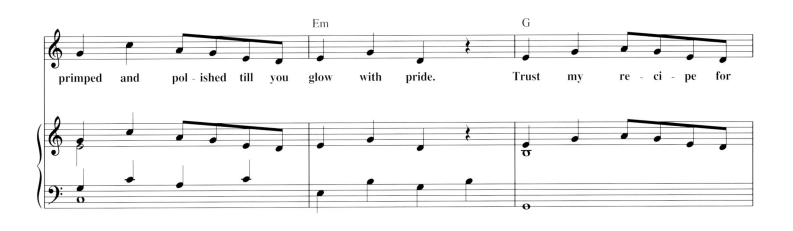

primped and pol - ished till you glow with pride. Trust my re - ci - pe for

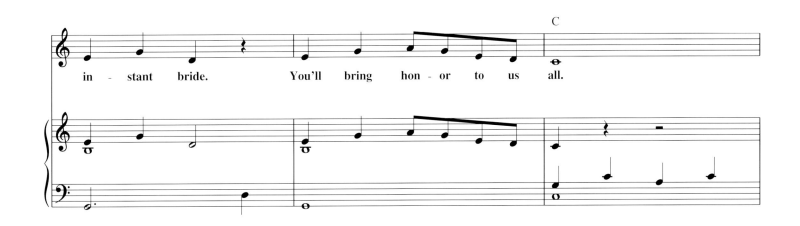

in - stant bride. You'll bring hon - or to us all.

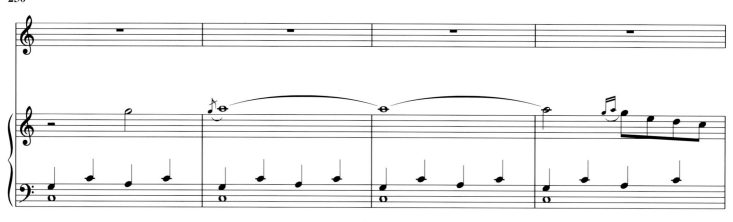

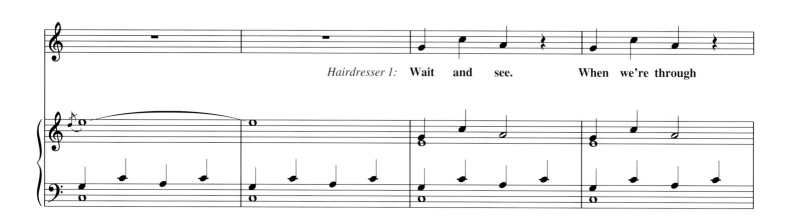

Hairdresser 1: **Wait and see.** **When we're through**

Hairdresser 2: **boys will glad - ly go to war for you.** *Hairdresser 1:* **With good** *Hairdresser 2:* **for - tune and a**

Hairdressers 1, 2 & Fa Li: **great hair - do you'll bring hon - or to us all.**

232

Honor To Us All
From Walt Disney Pictures' *Mulan*

Music by Matthew Wilder
Lyrics by David Zippel

Bather:	This is what you give me to work with.
	Well, honey, I've seen worse.
	We're going to turn this sow's ear into a silk purse.
	We'll have you washed and dried,
	Primped and polished till you glow with pride.
	Trust my recipe for instant bride.
	You'll bring honor to us all.
Hairdresser 1:	Wait and see. When we're through
Hairdresser 2:	Boys will gladly go to war for you.
Hairdresser 1:	With good
Hairdresser 2:	Fortune and a great hairdo
Hairdresser 1, 2 & Fa Li:	You'll bring honor to us all.
All:	A girl can bring her family great honor in one way -
	By striking a good match, and this could be the day.
Dressmaker 1:	Men want girls with good taste,
Dressmaker 2:	Calm,
Fa Li:	Obedient,
Dressmaker 1:	Who work fast-paced,
Fa Li:	With good breeding
Dressmaker 2:	And a tiny waist.
Dressmaker 1, 2 & Fa Li:	You'll bring honor to us all.
Women:	We all must serve our Emperor who guards us from the Huns;
	A man by bearing arms, a girl by bearing sons.
	When we're through, you can't fail, like a lotus
	Blossom soft and pale.
	How could any fellow say, "No sale"?
	You'll bring honor to us all.
Fa Li:	(Spoken:) *There, you're ready.*
Grandmother Fa:	(Spoken:) *Not yet. An apple for serenity...A pendant for balance...*
	(Sung:) Beads of jade for beauty.
	You must proudly show it.
	Now add a cricket just for luck *and even you can't blow it.*
Mulan:	Ancestors, hear my plea. Help me not to make a
	Fool of me and to not uproot my family tree.
	Keep my father standing tall.
Young Girls & Mulan:	Scarier than the undertaker, we are meeting our matchmaker.
All:	Destiny, guard our girls and our future as it fast unfurls.
	Please look kindly on these cultured pearls,
	Each a perfect porcelain doll.
	Please bring honor to us.
	Please bring honor to us.
	Please bring honor to us.
	Please bring honor to us.
	Please bring honor to us all.

Reflection

From Walt Disney Pictures' *Mulan*

Music by MATTHEW WILDER
Lyrics by DAVID ZIPPEL

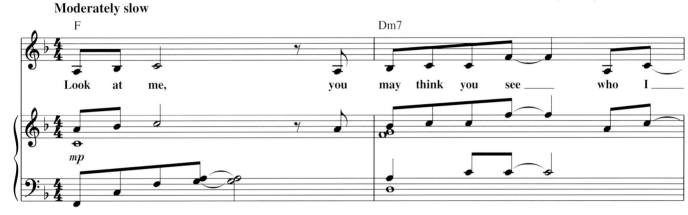

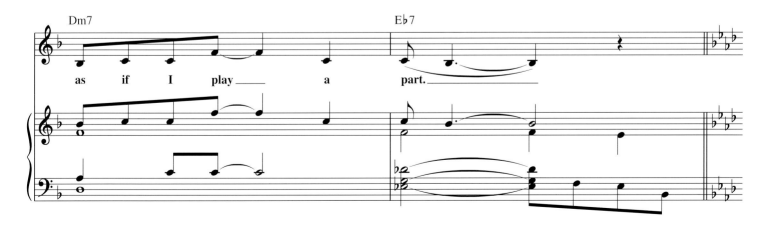

Look at me, you may think you see who I really am, but you'll nev-er know me. Ev-'ry day it's as if I play a part.

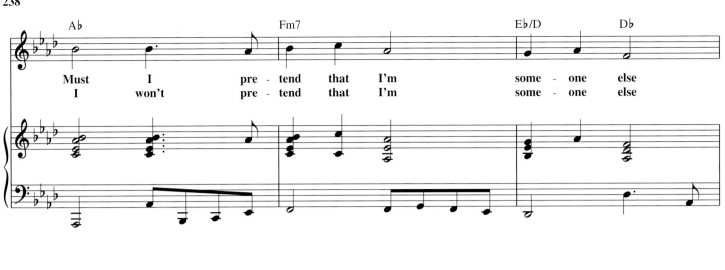

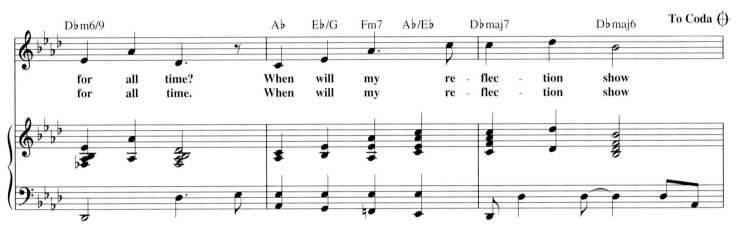

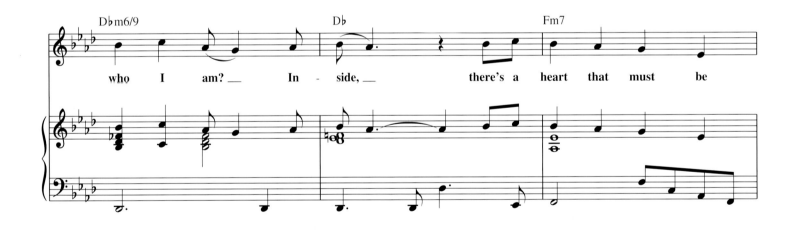

Old Yeller
From Walt Disney's *Old Yeller*

Words by GIL GEORGE
Music by OLIVER WALLACE

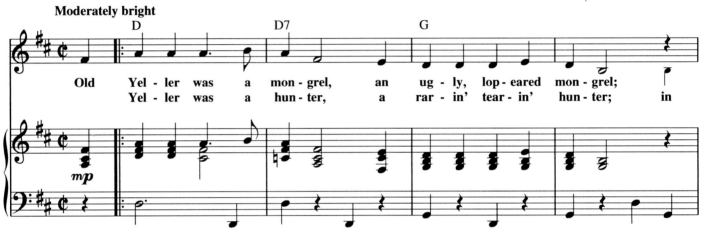

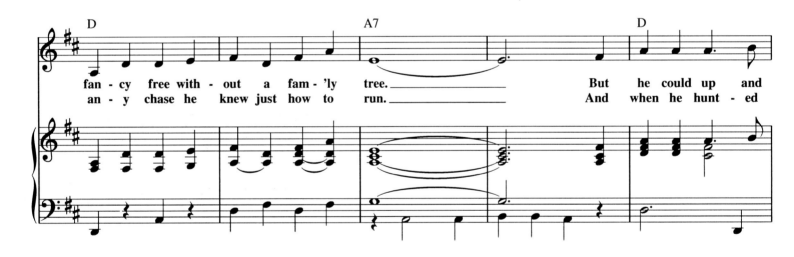

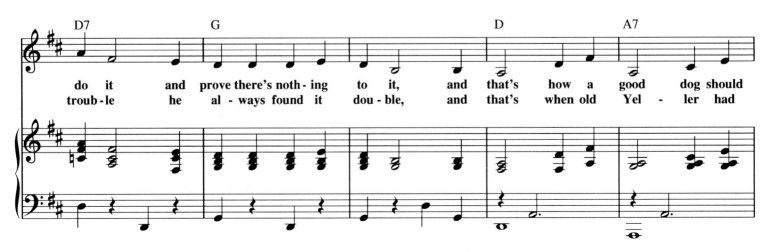

Let's Get Together

From Walt Disney's *The Parent Trap*

Words and Music by RICHARD M. SHERMAN
and ROBERT B. SHERMAN

Castle In Spain

From Walt Disney's *Babes In Toyland*

Words by MEL LEVEN
Music by GEORGE BRUNS

Lyrics:

In our cas-tle in Spain ___ you'll be
mort-gage and lease ___ I will
you must a-gree ___ that it

liv-ing rent free. ___ Ev - 'ry
re - val - u - ate. ___ And for
makes your head whirl ___ to be

cap - i - tal gain ___ you'll share with
you I'll in - crease ___ their share in - t'rest
mar - ry - ing me, ___ you luck - y

Fortuosity

From Walt Disney's *The Happiest Millionaire*

Words and Music by RICHARD M. SHERMAN
and ROBERT B. SHERMAN

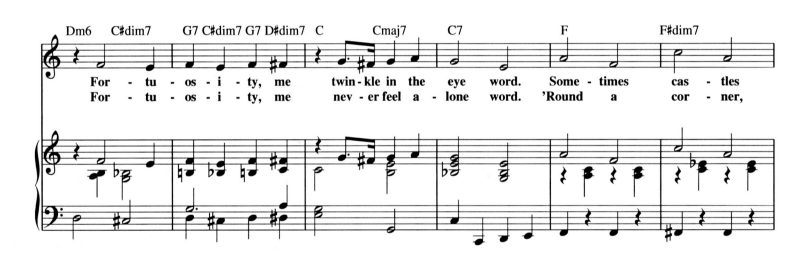

250

Seize The Day

From Walt Disney's *Newsies*

Music by ALAN MENKEN
Lyrics by JACK FELDMAN

Hymn-like

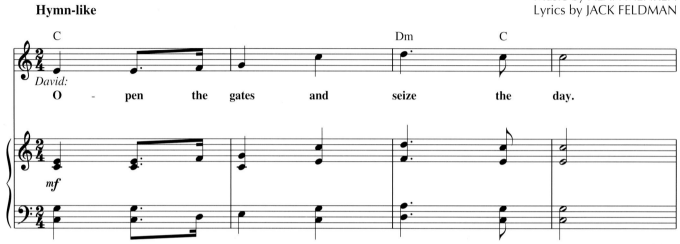

David: O - pen the gates and seize the day.

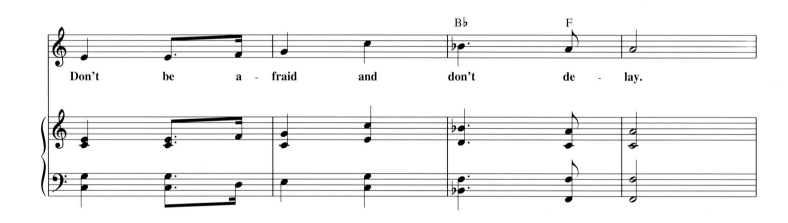

Don't be a - fraid and don't de - lay.

Noth - ing can break us. No one can make us

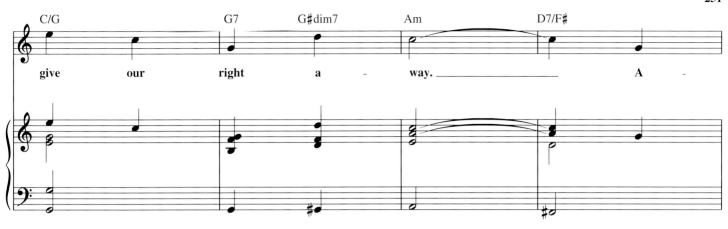

give our right a - way._____ A -

Brightly

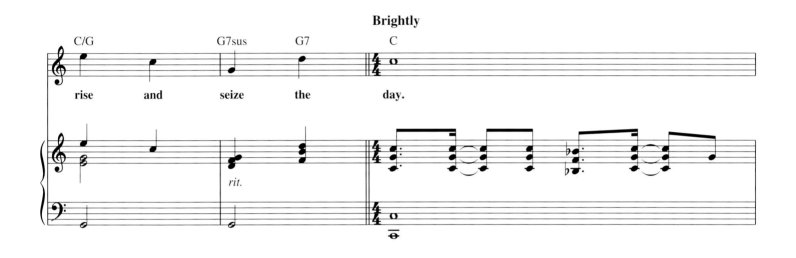

rise and seize the day.

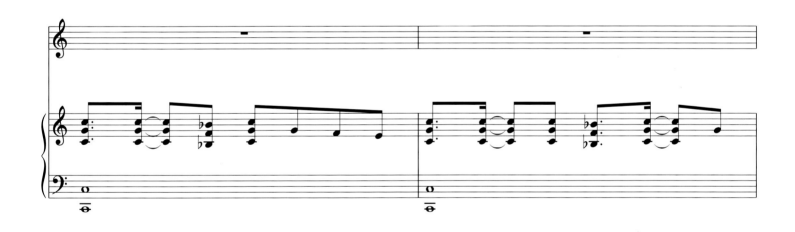

David: **Now is the time to seize the day.**

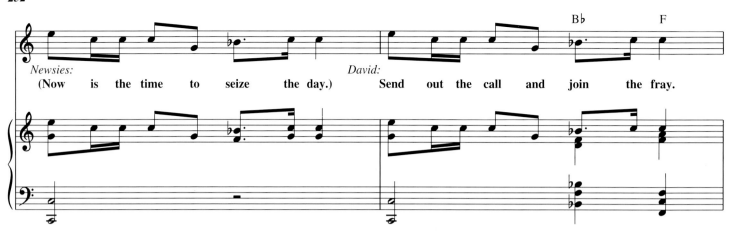

Newsies:
(Now is the time to seize the day.)

David:
Send out the call and join the fray.

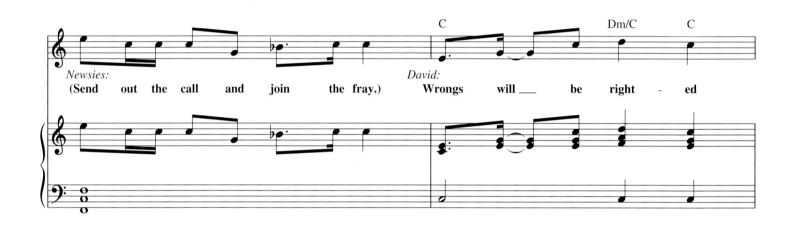

Newsies:
(Send out the call and join the fray.)

David:
Wrongs will ___ be right - ed

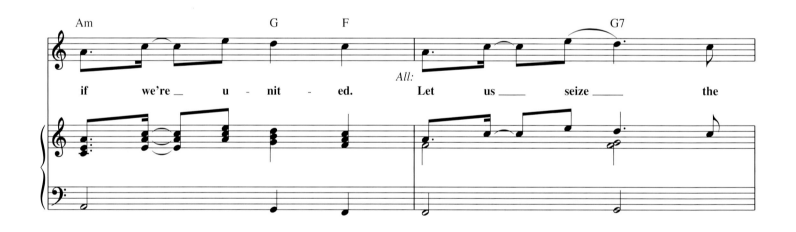

if we're ___ u - nit - ed.

All:
Let us ___ seize ___ the

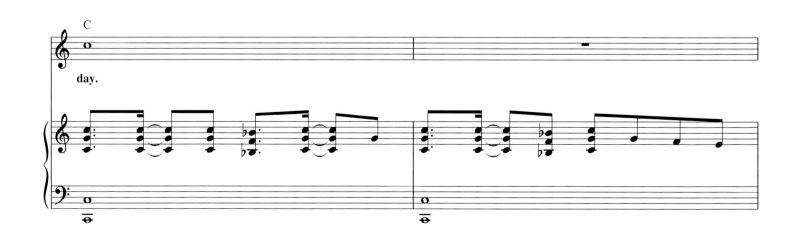

day.

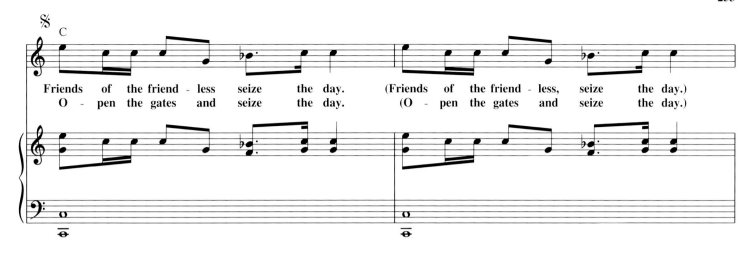

Friends of the friend - less seize the day. (Friends of the friend - less, seize the day.)
O - pen the gates and seize the day. (O - pen the gates and seize the day.)

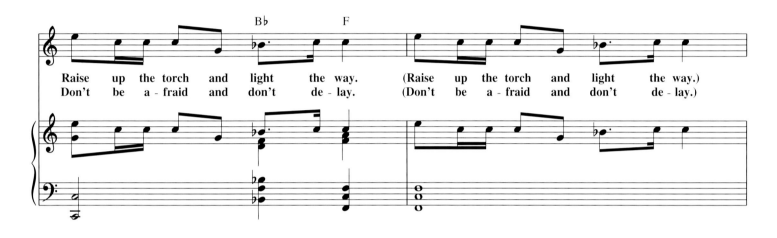

Raise up the torch and light the way. (Raise up the torch and light the way.)
Don't be a - fraid and don't de - lay. (Don't be a - fraid and don't de - lay.)

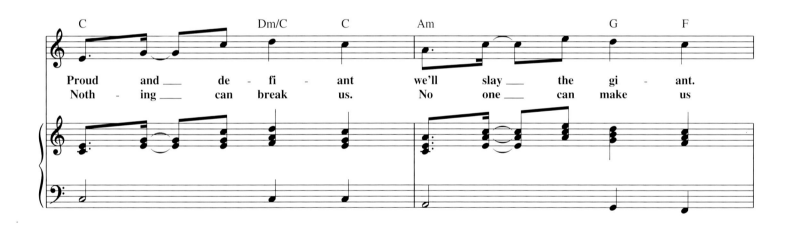

Proud and ___ de - fi - ant we'll slay ___ the gi - ant.
Noth - ing ___ can break us. No one ___ can make us

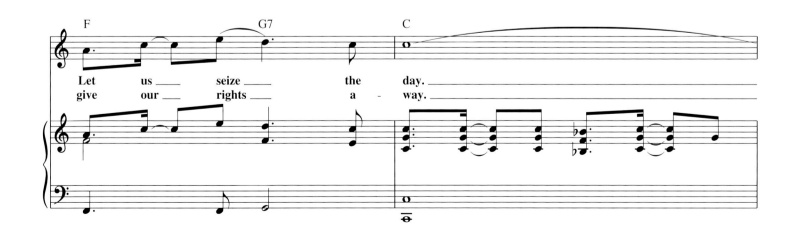

Let us ___ seize ___ the day. ___
give our ___ rights ___ a - way. ___

254

The Ballad Of Davy Crockett

From Walt Disney's
Davy Crockett

Words by TOM BLACKBURN
Music by GEORGE BRUNS

Moderately

1. Born on a moun-tain top in Ten - nes - see, green - est state in the land of the free, raised in the woods so's he knew ev -'ry tree, kilt him a b'ar when he was on - ly three. Da - vy, Da - vy Crock-ett, king of the wild fron -
2. eigh - teen - thir - teen the Creeks up - rose, addin' redskin arrows to the coun - try's woes. Now, In - jun fightin' is some - thin' he knows, so he shoul-ders his rifle an' off he goes. Da - vy, Da - vy Crock-ett, the man who don't know
3. Off through the woods he's a marchin' a - long, makin' up yarns an' a - sing - in' a song, itch - in' fer fightin' an' right - in' a wrong, he's ringy as a b'ar an' twict as strong. Da - vy, Da - vy Crock-ett, the buck - skin buc - ca -
4. -17. *(See additional lyrics)*

Additional Lyrics

4. Andy Jackson is our gen'ral's name,
   his reg'lar soldiers we'll put to shame.
   Them redskin varmints us Volunteers'll tame,
   'cause we got the guns with the sure-fire aim.
   Davy—Davy Crockett, the champion of us all!

5. Headed back to war from the ol' home place,
   but Red Stick was leadin' a merry chase,
   fightin' an' burnin' at a devil's pace
   south to the swamps on the Florida Trace.
   Davy—Davy Crockett, trackin' the redskins down!

6. Fought single-handed through the Injun War
   till the Creeks was whipped an' peace was in store.
   An' while he was handlin' this risky chore,
   made hisself a legend for evermore.
   Davy—Davy Crockett, king of the wild frontier!

7. He give his word an' he give his hand
   that his Injun friends could keep their land.
   An' the rest of his life he took the stand
   that justice was due every redskin band.
   Davy—Davy Crockett, holdin' his promise dear!

8. Home fer the winter with his family,
   happy as squirrels in the ol' gum tree,
   bein' the father he wanted to be,
   close to his boys as the pod an' the pea.
   Davy—Davy Crockett, holdin' his young 'uns dear!

9. But the ice went out an' the warm winds came
   an' the meltin' snow showed tracks of game.
   An' the flowers of Spring filled the woods with flame,
   an' all of a sudden life got too tame.
   Davy—Davy Crockett, headin' on West again!

10. Off through the woods we're ridin' along,
    makin' up yarns an' singin' a song.
    He's ringy as a b'ar an' twict as strong,
    an' knows he's right 'cause he ain' often wrong.
    Davy—Davy Crockett, the man who don't know fear!

11. Lookin' fer a place where the air smells clean,
    where the trees is tall an' the grass is green,
    where the fish is fat in an untouched stream,
    an' the teemin' woods is a hunter's dream.
    Davy—Davy Crockett, lookin' fer Paradise!

12. Now he's lost his love an' his grief was gall,
    in his heart he wanted to leave it all,
    an' lose himself in the forests tall,
    but he answered instead his country's call.
    Davy—Davy Crockett, beginnin' his campaign!

13. Needin' his help they didn't vote blind.
    They put in Davy 'cause he was their kind,
    sent up to Nashville the best they could find,
    a fightin' spirit an' a thinkin' mind.
    Davy—Davy Crockett, choice of the whole frontier!

14. The votes were counted an' he won hands down,
    so they sent him off to Washin'ton town
    with his best dress suit still his buckskins brown,
    a livin' legend of growin' renown.
    Davy—Davy Crockett, the Canebrake Congressman!

15. He went off to Congress an' served a spell,
    fixin' up the Gover'ments an' laws as well,
    took over Washin'ton so we heered tell
    an' patched up the crack in the Liberty Bell.
    Davy—Davy Crockett, seein' his duty clear!

16. Him an' his jokes travelled all through the land,
    an' his speeches made him friends to beat the band.
    His politickin' was their favorite brand
    an' everyone wanted to shake his hand.
    Davy—Davy Crockett, helpin' his legend grow!

17. He knew when he spoke he sounded the knell
    of his hopes for White House an' fame as well.
    But he spoke out strong so hist'ry books tell
    an' patched up the crack in the Liberty Bell.
    Davy—Davy Crockett, seein' his duty clear!

Mickey Mouse March

From Walt Disney's *The Mickey Mouse Club*

Words and Music by
JIMMIE DODD

It's A Small World

From Disneyland and Walt Disney World's
It's A Small World

Words and Music by RICHARD M. SHERMAN
and ROBERT B. SHERMAN

Yo Ho
(A Pirate's Life For Me)
From Disneyland and Walt Disney World's
Pirates Of The Caribbean

Words by XAVIER ATENCIO
Music by GEORGE BRUNS

In a robust manner

Yo ho, yo ho, a pi-rate's life for me. We
Yo ho, yo ho, a pi-rate's life for me. We
Yo ho, yo ho, a pi-rate's life for me. We

pil-lage, plun-der, we ri-fle and loot. Drink up me 'eart-ies, yo ho. We
ex-tort and pil-fer, we filch and sack. Drink up me 'eart-ies, yo ho. Ma-
kin-dle and char and in-flame and ig-nite. Drink up me 'eart-ies, yo ho. We

kid-nap and rav-age and don't give a hoot. Drink up me 'eart-ies, yo ho.
raud and em-bez-zle and e-ven high-jack. Drink up me 'eart-ies, yo ho.
burn up the cit-y, we're real-ly a fright. Drink

SONG INDEX